The Blackman's Champion

Black Women, this is a Tribute: Thanks for Everything!

Maurice I. Crawford

CONTENTS

INTRODUCTION

The timeless history of Black Americans is wrought with racism and oppression. At the turn of the last century, African Americans were considered 3/5ths of a person by the Constitution—they had no rights and no voice. At this time, Black American women saw themselves as innately strong—nurturing their families, raising their children to value education and hard work, and volunteering in their communities.

In the 20th century, a major transformation took place. The laws regarding the treatment of Black individuals were completely revamped and updated to be more egalitarian; however, this new law was not applied equally to Black women. Black women continued to be criticized for being "sexually loose" when a majority of them chose to continue their family responsibilities rather than work outside the home. This meant that they were still considered to be unchaste and immoral by white society and thus not viewed as deserving of their rights or worthiness as human beings.

Throughout history, your stories are the threads that weave together the resilience, strength, and beauty of the Black community. Today, we shine a light on the unsung heroines—the Black women who have stood tall, unyielding in the face of centuries of turmoil, triumph, and societal evolution. Your contributions, often overlooked, have been the heartbeat of our collective journey.

For too long, the narrative has focused on the struggles and triumphs of the Black man, and rightfully so. Yet, behind every great Black man, there stands an extraordinary Black woman. Your strength has been the bedrock upon which our community has built its foundation. Through the storms of history, you have been the steady force, the unwavering pillar that sustains and uplifts.

In times of adversity, it is your spirit that has shone brightly, guiding us through the darkest hours. Whether it be the fight for civil rights, the quest for education and equality, or the daily battles against systemic injustices, your resilience has been a beacon of hope. Your unwavering commitment to family, community, and justice has shaped the narrative of our shared history.

You are the nurturers, the educators, the activists, and the trailblazers. From the Civil Rights Movement to the present day, your voices have echoed in the halls of change. Your hands have built bridges, forged paths, and paved the way for future generations. In boardrooms, classrooms, and community centers, your impact is immeasurable.

Your journey has been one of strength in the face of adversity, of triumphs carved out of the rock of struggle. It's a story that deserves to be told, understood, and celebrated.

Through the ebbs and flows of time, your influence has been like a steady river, shaping and nourishing the roots of the Black community. It's a multifaceted role that goes beyond the surface, beyond what meets the eye. "Resilience and Reverence" seeks to explore and illuminate those dimensions—the struggles you've faced, the victories you've claimed, and the enduring impact you've had on the Black community and the nation as a whole.

Your resilience, like a diamond forged under pressure, has not only sustained but also propelled the Black man forward. In your struggles, there is strength, and in your victories, there is inspiration. Your contributions have been the backbone of a community—the silent force that has shaped destinies and shifted the course of history.

The Strength of Black Women in America:

Just like any group of individuals, Black women come in various shapes, sizes, and attitudes. Yet, there's no denying that society has placed a unique set of obstacles in front of them. Still, they have become a teeny-tiny bit successful in, well, just about every single industry. Name it, they've got it!

The Influence of Black Women Throughout History:

Just when you thought Black women were only good for twerking and gossiping, a quick dive into history challenges your sophisticated perspectives. Black women have made massive strides, be it in art, politics, or the business world. And if you think it's just in recent times, darling, these women have been defying gravity since the days of slavery!

This book is a celebration of you—your strength, your wisdom, and your grace. It's an affirmation of the power that resides within each of you and a recognition of the collective force that binds you together. "Resilience and Reverence" is a tribute to the queens who have weathered storms and emerged with crowns unscathed.

As we delve into this comprehensive journey, let it be a

mirror reflecting the beauty of your spirit, the depth of your character, and the profound impact you've had on the Black community and the nation. Your story is not just a chapter; it's a testament to the enduring power of Black women—the architects of resilience, the custodians of reverence.

As we celebrate your strength, we recognize the importance of amplifying your voices and acknowledging the multifaceted roles you play. You are not just supporting characters in the story of the Black community; you are the protagonists, the storytellers, and the architects of our shared destiny.

To every Black woman who has faced adversity with grace, who has triumphed against the odds, and who continues to inspire us all, we salute you. Your strength is not only unsung but undeniable. It is a force that has shaped history and will undoubtedly continue to do so.

"The Blackman's Champion" is not just a title; it's a recognition, a nod of appreciation, and a celebration of the Black woman's journey. It's a tribute to the queens who have shaped our past, are shaping our present, and will undoubtedly shape our future. Your strength is our strength, and your story is our story. Let us revel in it, honor it, and pass it on, ensuring that your contributions are never again unsung.

CHAPTER 1: INVISIBLE STRENGTHS: UNVEILING THE FOUNDATION OF BLACK WOMEN

Unveiling the unseen power, you say? Well, let me tell you a whimsical secret: Black women have been a force to be reckoned with throughout history. Now, don't confuse it with the fictional Wonder Woman's power or even Harry Potter's magic wand, for it's something much deeper and more genuine. We're talking about the mind-boggling strength of spirit and perseverance that have defined them for centuries. Yes, that's right—this is the essence of resilience and spiritual legacy!

Now that we have set the stage, let's peek through keyholes and delve into this magnificent journey of rediscovering the power that lies within Black women. Fasten your imaginary seatbelts, open your minds and hearts, and let's celebrate the unbroken legacy of resilience together. After all, who doesn't love a fabulous tribute to some powerful ladies?

As our little adventure unfolds, we'll encounter renowned spiritualists like Luisah Teish, who embarked on an incredible journey to uncover the roots of Black women's spirituality in New Orleans. Spoiler alert: we'll also discuss the oh-so-mysterious Voodoo traditions and their connection to the amazing Black women's resilience.

And, speaking of resilience, we cannot overlook the storm-breaker stereotype of the "strong Black woman." Breaking the chains, we shall dig into the importance of vulnerability and how embracing weakness is the key to maintaining Black women's physical and emotional well-being.

Hold on tight as we time-travel and revisit the exceptional and awe-inspiring journey of Black women, from the sad days of slavery to the heights of the civil rights movement. Be prepared to encounter strong spirits and unbreakable wills as we reveal the untold stories of resilience.

Oh, how could we forget about the powerful pen that has immortalized Black women's spirits in literature? We'll tip our hats to literary geniuses like Hurston, Shange, and Morrison, who, through their masterpieces, have provided a testament to Black women's unyielding resilience and vibrant spirituality.

And finally, our little extravaganza will culminate in the exploration of self-definition and the unimaginable power that lies within. So, get ready to witness the marvelous journey of spiritual growth and how embracing one's true self can pave the way to resilience and ultimate divinity.

Spiritual Backbone: Black Women and Faith

There's always something that runs deep within the soul of our kings: their spiritual backbone. In the journey of life, faith plays a monumental role in shaping the character and resilience of our Black men.

Black women are the pillars of strength that uphold our communities. Your unwavering faith has been the anchor in the storm, providing a safe harbor for our brothers. As we navigate the complexities of the world, it's crucial to recognize the profound connection between Black women and the spiritual well-being of Black men.

Black men draw strength from the spiritual fortitude that radiates from you. Your prayers, your rituals, and your connection to something greater than yourselves inspire a sense of purpose and belonging in the hearts of our Black men. In the mosaic of our culture, faith intertwines with resilience, creating a powerful synergy that fuels the pursuit of justice, equality, and prosperity.

As the heartbeat of our families, Black women nurture not only the bodies and minds but also the spirits of Black men. Your ability to instill values, morals, and a sense of purpose is unparalleled. In a world that often seeks to diminish the essence of our people, your faith becomes a guiding light, leading our men toward self-discovery, self-love, and a profound understanding of their place in the universe.

Black women, you are the embodiment of spirituality in its purest form. Your resilience in the face of adversity, your ability to find strength in vulnerability, and your commitment to building a legacy of love and faith are the threads that weave the fabric of our communities.

So, let's continue to uplift, support, and cherish one another. Your spirituality is not just a personal journey; it is a beacon that guides our men through the darkest nights and toward the brightest days. Together, as partners on this spiritual journey, let's cultivate a legacy of faith, love, and strength that will echo through generations.

Now, some of you might think, "A graveyard? Really?!" Yep, you heard it right. But it's not just any graveyard she visited. She ventured into the Voodoo Queen's crypt! It's not the usual sightseeing destination, I agree. But Louisa Teish deviates from the usual and does an intricate 'Sherlock Holmes' on the Voodoo Tradition! Going around with her detective hat on, she chats up with the lady's neighbors and even connects with her spirit to bring a refreshing look at Black women's Voodoo tradition.

And then there's Christianity. Now, describing how Black women embrace their divinity and spirituality through Christianity is as complex as explaining why pizza is round but comes in a square box and is served in triangles. (Yeah, wrap your brain around that one.) But stick with me here. Remember your grandmother praying fervently as if she were having a heart-to-heart with God himself? Or those whispers about "roots" and "conjuring" you accidentally overheard during family gatherings? Those aren't just hocus-pocus or old wives' tales. They're a living, breathing part of the vibrant, rich spiritual history of Black women.

No matter how many memes we see on social media joking about grandmas thumping their Bibles and shouting "Hallelujah!" in the pulpit, Black women's relationship with God runs deeper than captcha codes and is authentically real. It's like a VIP members-only club where God's Holy Spirit and Black women kick it together, with the Holy Spirit offering a divine margarita of rest, strength, and resilience.

Melissa Harris-Perry, in her moonlighting role as a political scientist, not just the news anchor dolling out MSNBC news, brings to light how Black women can bare their souls, confess their vulnerabilities, and seek authenticity through religious faith. They come to God, not seeking a cheap 5-minute spa treatment, but to seriously "lay their burdens down." It's like being in wrist-locks and foot-binds all day and finally letting loose, allowing the Lord to carry your weight and fight your battles.

So, think of it this way, folks. Instead of dropping a quarter in the wishing well and expecting miracles, they're dropping their prayers on the altar and expecting metamorphosis.

Black Women and Vulnerability: Breaking Stereotypes

We all come across stereotypes, some more than others. The strong, silent type. The blonde airhead. The geek. Each boasts its own sparkling umbrella of assumptions and judgments. Well, buckle up because we are about to obliterate one major stereotype that's faithfully latched onto Black women like a stubborn tick—the strong Black woman.

This line of thinking paints a picture of invulnerability. She is supposed to be a pocket-sized superhero, battling all of life's nuances head-on, ideally without shedding a single tear. It's like she has an unlimited supply of energy drinks and a playlist of "Eye of the Tiger" on repeat. The idea is that the Black woman must bear the brunt for everyone—men, children, even life itself—without batting an eye. Weeping? That's for the faint-hearted, right?

Black women might be good at multitasking, but they are not production machines. They are not built to give birth to a baby and harvest a field on the same day, and if they were, well, I'd say that's one heck of a Labor Day! Nor are they designed to move from a sorrowful widow to a factory worker overnight.

Moving on to health, they say, "A woman's place is in the house... and Senate," but perhaps we should add 'therapy' in there too. Talking about weakness, having insecurities, and admitting fear is considered taboo. Black women are humans, not superheroes. They need someone to hold their hand, lend an ear, and pass a tissue (or two). Damsels in distress may be an outdated stereotype, but everyone needs rescuing sometimes, even the so-called strong ones.

Admitting vulnerability isn't so much about showing your kryptonite as it is about embracing the human spirit in its entirety. It's not about submitting to the negative chatter in our heads; it's about declaring war on it by saying it out loud. Contrary to the clichéd belief, letting out those bottled emotions is not akin to opening Pandora's box. It's a step towards healing—a tap on the shoulder of inner strength.

Vulnerability is not a sign of weaker mental health, but quite the opposite. It's the golden key that unlocks the treasure of inner peace and well-being. It holds the potential to transform the strong Black woman stereotype into an empowered Black woman reality. And we are not talking about the glossy, picture-perfect empowerment that social media throws at us; it's raw, real, and, most importantly, relatable.

Easier said than done, I hear you say. However, the first step is acknowledging the problem. Then comes the hard part, the battlefield, where you fight the demons of stereotypes and societal expectations. Nevertheless, remember that it's a journey, and who doesn't love a good journey, especially one with a victorious and mentally healthier outcome? You are waiting at the end, waving a flag of triumph, and probably sipping a well-deserved mojito too.

So, here's to shattering stereotypes, embracing vulnerabilities, and celebrating the unharnessed power of being human. After all, even superheroes need to hang up their capes sometimes.

The Resilient Survivors of History

I wish you could see the gleam in my eyes right now, as I'm all set to take you on a grittily phenomenal journey of Black women, a tale that flows right from the infernal, iron-ringed shackles of slavery to the gallantly audacious era of the civil rights movement.

Imagine this! A time when 'rights' was just a word that dared not creep into a Black woman's lexicon. Hell, even being labeled a "woman" was thought to be an overstatement. They got their boarding passes for the 'Transatlantic Slave-Ship' Express, definitely not as a choice but painfully by force, from Africa to the Americas. Assumptions might paint the slavery period as a linear period of oppression and violation of Black women. Well, not to burst that bubble, but it sure wasn't just about whipping, lynching, or sexual exploitation. Get that monocle off; history isn't that bland!

However, life isn't all rainbows and unicorns. While these women powered through gut-wrenching atrocities, they never let their spirit—their true spirit—disappear, much like a queen who, despite losing her crown, never lets her dignity falter. They learned to cultivate their strength, resilience, and unbroken spirit amidst heavy trials and cascading prejudice. This 'unbroken spirit' is the brand I assure you to adorn with no baseless warranties.

Honey, not to break your heart, but even after the legal abolishment of slavery in 1865, the soot of discrimination didn't vanish! Life as a Black woman was like a movie with an unending climax, making the audience wonder, "When is the actual turning point going to happen?" Fast forward to the civil rights movement era, thrown into a turbulent sea of political strife, armed with Manual No. 2 (Manual No. 1 was losing effectiveness), these gallant soldiers rose up for cause, color, and community.

During this era, their hair turned a bit grayer, their eyes exhausted but hopeful, and their hearts pounding with passion. They took to the streets, not simply as 'protestors' but as embodiments of the veritable force of nature. Their voice echoed through valleys and cities, braiding itself inseparably into the annals of history. They chose to rise every time they were pushed down.

Just imagine the audacity of Black women to use calamity not as a period but as a comma in their chapters of resistance, to rise higher every time they were nudged lower. Their journey of resilience and struggle is an unsung symphony with as many heroes as there are stars in the night sky. How about we keep the lights of their spirit brightly glowing till eternity and a day more?

Creation in Literature: A Testament to Black Women's Spirit

Literature is indeed the perfect stage for our heroines to flourish and bask in the limelight that they, without question, deserve.

Let's begin our literary rendezvous with the iconic Zora Neale Hurston, whose pen exalted Black women like never before. Through her journey, Hurston gave voice to marginalized African American women and allowed them to take charge of their narrative in the most Herculean way possible. Indeed, she believed in the sassy power of storytelling as a means to break cultural barriers and to pioneer real and lasting change. Brava, Hurston!

Next, we have Ntozake Shange, the trailblazing author responsible for the beautifully provocative and revolutionary "For Colored Girls Who Have Considered Suicide/When The Rainbow Is Enuf." Shange explored themes of empowerment, self-love, and reclaiming the Black female identity through her groundbreaking choreography.

Like a sorceress, she weaved her words and characters in such an enigmatic yet liberating way, leaving her audience more than simply spellbound.

Last but definitely not least, we have the maestro herself, Ms. Toni Morrison. The queen of literary flare, Morrison, crafted mesmerizing stories that unapologetically embraced the vast complexities and nuances attached to Black womanhood. From novels like "Beloved" to "Sula," she breathed life into characters who were unstoppably defiant, effortlessly fascinating, and undeniably human.

Now that we've all had our breaths taken away by these stunning masterpieces, here's another secret ingredient that ties them all together: storytelling as resistance. Yes, you heard it right—it's like a poetic rebellion just waiting to happen!

So, while our literary divas reveled in the magic of prose, they also made a powerful statement through their narratives. By celebrating Black women and embracing their inner beauty, power, and undeniable spirit, these authors were steadily crushing age-old stereotypes imposed by society.

Storytelling enabled these larger-than-life authors to challenge the status quo, crush expectations, and inspire generations to rewrite the rules. These women painted the literary canvas with characters that embodied strength, resilience, and a fierce passion for self-discovery and, in doing so, perpetuated the reality that Black women need not be confined by social or cultural constructs. It's like literary emancipation, and it feels so good, doesn't it?

In their varying yet equally brilliant ways, Hurston, Shange, and Morrison have presented the world with an invaluable gift—a timeless tribute to the resilience and spiritual legacy of Black women. Through their craft, they gave voice to the voiceless and paved the way for future generations to embrace the power of self-definition.

So, the next time you find yourself swept away by the whirlwind of their words, take a moment to marvel at the revolutionary spirit that echoes through their literary masterpieces. As they effortlessly bend and break conventions, these extraordinary authors remind us that our voices matter and our stories are nothing short of magic.

And with that, our literary journey comes to an end (for now). As we bid farewell to the enchanting realms of Hurston, Shange, and Morrison, always remember: Keep spinning your own stories, embracing your authentic selves with pride. Because if there's one thing we can all take away from these queens of the pen, it's that our voices truly do hold the power to change the world.

Self-Definition: Embracing the Power of Self

The sweet power of self-definition is like that first bite of chocolate after a long day, the warm hug of a loved one, or the sudden realization that, yes, you are indeed wearing the perfect outfit.

Now, you might wonder, "What does self-definition have to do with our beloved Black women?" You see, the journey of reclaiming self through spiritual work is absolutely essential in their path to resilience, like avocado on toast.

The power of self-definition is all about saying "Adios!" "Au revoir!" "Sayonara!" or any other fancy goodbye you choose to the immediate assumptions and constrictions society places on Black women. Here's where the fascinating game of breaking stereotypes comes into play—a game Black women play masterfully, project heads up, and like true warriors, face mind-boggling assumptions that try to bind them.

And when we say breaking stereotypes, we don't mean just your run-of-the-mill, everyday type of breaking. This is like Thor smashing his hammer into the ground and creating the most fabulous rainbow bridge, to everyone's amazement. It's about overcoming objectification, flipping the script, and realizing who's the real superhero here. It's Black women.

Self-definition is a bicycle that'll take you places, but you need to put in some effort. The spokes of this bicycle consist of nothing else but the spiritual work that Black women dedicate themselves to. To truly understand self-definition, you must first understand the power of spirituality.

Feel your inner Sherlock Holmes tingling? Don't worry; we've got the magnifying glass and pipe all set to unravel this problem. Clever detectives that we are, a thorough look into the practices of spiritual work would reveal the incredible transformations it can bring to a soul weighed down by generational trauma and societal expectations bestowed upon one's shoulders.

What lies at the center of spiritual work is the unyielding quest for inner healing, overcoming external oppression, balancing the chaos within, and reclaiming the essence of who one truly is, like a phoenix rising from the ashes.

Black women are renowned for their spiritual perseverance. It's through this work that the path to resilience is paved with prayers, meditations, counseling sessions, and a deep, unwavering determination to overcome their struggles. You see, much like an onion, there are many layers to peel back, and spiritual work becomes the sharpest knife to cut through these tough exterior layers and reveal the most authentic, vulnerable self.

As the great American philosopher Beyoncé once sang, "I'm a grown woman; I can do whatever I want." This lyric serves as a mantra for all Black women who find themselves trapped in a cage of limiting stereotypes. They embrace their power of self-definition, shatter the cage with a mighty roar, and dance to the melodious tunes of their newfound resilience.

By harnessing the power of spiritual work, they continue to write the narrative of their lives with an impeccable flair for rising above adversity, like Olympic high jumpers creating new records, defying gravity, and societal constraints alike.

In the end, Black women's resilient spirit is truly a testament to their strength, and we can't help but stand in awe of their sheer power to overcome and revolutionize the world around them, leap by mesmerizing leap. Now, if only we could borrow an ounce of that unyielding resilience for our next downward spiral into procrastination, am I right?

CHAPTER 2: LEGACY OF RESILIENCE: TRACING THE JOURNEY FROM ANCESTRAL ROOTS TO MODERN CHALLENGES OF BLACK WOMEN

You may not realize it, but the roots of Black women go way back to when their ancestors helped shape their identities by being the epitome of courage and survival. Hanging onto their family stories like the perfect chocolate chip cookie recipe, they established the narrative that resilience was their middle name. Throughout history, these women have faced unprecedented challenges and emerged victorious, proving that they've got that fierceness running through their veins.

Speaking of fierceness, let's talk about something that definitely deserves a standing ovation: generational resilience. Through a saga of bravery, Black women have passed on their values of strength, determination, and perseverance from generation to generation, creating a tenacious lineage ready to conquer any obstacle in their way. Who doesn't love a tear-jerking movie where the heroine overcomes all odds?

As we talk about this exhilarating ride of their lives, we need to take a moment to address a villain who tried (and failed miserably, mind you) to bring these women down to settler colonialism. These Eurocentric bullies tried their best to impose their hegemonic standards on Black women, but guess what? Like the superheroes in shiny armor, these ladies persisted and built their identities amidst adversity.

Now that we've met one villain, let's meet another one: patriarchal societal constructs. Black women had to confront a system that had cornered them into the "inferior" mold. But in a jaw-dropping plot twist, they shattered these chains and decided to create their beautiful identities based on their unique history, values, and culture. Take a moment to appreciate this sass, folks.

Like a gripping saga, our journey now lands us in the present day, where modern challenges lie in the paths of Black women. Racial and gender disparities are omnipresent and seem committed to holding them back, but these indomitable women continue their relentless struggle for equity and inclusion. If I were you, I would not bet against them!

It's time to pay homage to these resilient Black women who, against all odds, continue to celebrate their strength and carve their well-deserved space into our world. Raising a toast to the warriors who slayed their way through discrimination, prejudice, and stereotypes and emerged as the champions they are.

Tracing Ancestral Roots

Digging into the roots of the African diaspora, we find a complex web of resilience, heartache, and triumph. Our ancestral roots reveal a saga of surviving the tumultuous waters of history with the guidance and wisdom of our past. And now, let's embark on a fruitful journey to unearth the enigma of our ancestors, who managed to turn this rollercoaster of a journey into a timeless story of resilience.

You see, our dear ancestors had a proclivity for leaving behind droplets of wisdom for us to sponge up in our eternal quest for identity. Like breadcrumbs leading us back to our roots, our ancestors help shape our modern-day identity through the cryptic language of spirituality, intuition, and clues. It's as if they've pulled up a chair at our metaphysical dinner table, ready to chow down on nutritious tales of endurance and strength. And boy, is it a feast!

It is now our prerogative to put on our detective hats and decipher the ciphers left behind by our beloved ancestors. Without the clues they sprinkle throughout our lives, we may be left wandering aimlessly in the wilderness of our identities. Thankfully, albeit somewhat enigmatic, we have their guidance to light our way through the dark corridors of self-discovery. So, let's raise a glass to our ancestors, for their legacy speaks to our souls.

Our ancestral ties remind us that although stormy seas may surround us, we have the power to navigate the choppy waters and come out the other side even stronger. Let's take, for instance, the indomitable spirit and grace of our Black foremothers, who have bequeathed to us a steely resilience and a perpetual sense of hope.

These brave souls had to endure heart-wrenching sacrifice at the hands of colonialism and social constructs, yet they stood tall like majestic redwoods through it all. They unknowingly set the course for the modern-day Black woman to follow suit and conquer adversity through courage, strength, and sheer determination.

Now, as we channel the fortitude of our predecessors, our own triumphs echo through the generations and serve as a testament to the indomitable spirit shared by Black women. Our hearts are eternally tethered to our ancestors', vibrating with the same passion, love, and ferocity that have carried them through the most difficult times.

As we move forward through this journey, let's remember the wise words of our familiars: our identities are shaped by those who came before us, their stories embedded in the very fabric of our beings. Through their trials and tribulations, laughter, and sorrow, we understand who we truly are and who we aspire to become.

And just like that, we have made our way through the thickets of our ancestral terrain and emerged a little wiser, a little stronger, and a lot more inspired. So, as we continue to traverse the path of self-discovery, let's give a nod of gratitude to those who have come before us—for their guidance, love, and, most importantly, their unwavering resilience.

Cementing the Soil: Generational Resilience

If there were a "Who's Who" list of bravery, the names of our ancestral African women would roll off the tongue, filling pages faster than you can say "resilience." Their stories aren't just snippets of the past; they're the very DNA woven into our generational cloth.

Picture it: Their lives weren't sugar-coated unicorns and rainbow outings. It was like constant boxing matches, where they stood in one corner, fists tight, ready to fight for their dignity. Spare a thought for the hurdles they faced, shackled in chains by a ruthless system, and yet, were they unbending like a flapjack in a non-stick pan?

The ancestral Black women were your typical resilience OGs, introducing a new dimension to the 'never back down' philosophy. They held onto their native values as tight as my grandma held onto her secret chicken soup recipe. These values—a mix of great patience, relentless strength, and indomitable spirit—were their compass, guiding them through the darkest storms.

Instilling the values, let's think of our ancestral Black women as this incredible group of value-instilling Ninjas. Values were their secret weapon, their masterstroke. For them, values were more than just fancy words thrown around in discussion circles. The air they breathed—the driving force—etched a deep belief system in themselves and their descendants. They taught us to maneuver life's roller coaster while adding dignity, courage, a dash of resilience, and a sprinkling of respect to everything we do.

In a nutshell, they were master sculptors, ceaselessly chiseling, shaping, and molding generations. Their lessons? Just like that vintage wine, they've aged into time-defying golden lessons, echoing through the passage of time and still relevant today.

And let's not overlook that charming, cheeky trait they managed to instill- resilience. It's much like adding that secret spice to a dish that makes all the difference. They sprinkled resilience on us with the same enthusiasm. Remember, it's one thing to remain standing during a storm, but quite another to dance in the rain.

Suffice it to say, we're not just carrying their DNA; we're carrying their values, their battles, and their wins, and we're wearing all that heavy lifting like a badge of honor. So, next time you find yourself struggling, remember that you're a descendant of warriors and have the resilience of centuries flowing through you. Trust me, you've got this!

Black Women and Settler Colonialism

Settler colonialism is the unwanted guest whose influence still lingers like a stubborn party crasher. Oh yes, it's a charming acquaintance who meddled with the lives of Black women in a not-so-charming way. After all, who doesn't love dealing with the Eurocentric leadership? Well, Black women weren't exactly big fans.

In case you hadn't noticed, a substantial chunk of world history has been authored by and catered to white Europeans. So, when these scholarly scribes decided to paint Black women as inferior subjects in their Eurocentric narratives, it wasn't just a passing annoyance. As we reminisce on the rendezvous between Black women and settler colonialism, it's crucial to note that they have constantly grappled with Eurocentric hegemony, which became the unsolicited guru of societal norms and rules.

These norms dictated a Eurocentric worldview that disregarded Black women's heritage, teachings, and traditions. You know, things like self-worth, pride, and the genuine sense of identity one derives from one's ancestors. In response, Black women had two options:

either curl up into a ball of despair or rise against this absurdity.

Fortunately, the unshakable spirit and resilience of Black women didn't allow them to succumb to the Euro-trash propaganda. Instead, it sparked an unwavering determination to resist and challenge these alien philosophies. Contrary to popular belief in Eurocentric circles, these women persisted amidst adversity, unapologetically reclaiming spaces that had been snatched away from them.

In the face of cultural erasure, Black women kept their ancestral stories alive, playing cultural custodians with unwavering passion and responsibility. Such tales of heroism, wisdom, and adversity formed an invisible thread connecting them to their ancestors' strength. This enabled them to defy the Eurocentric hegemony, undauntedly demanding respect, dignity, and recognition.

But like with any Herculean task, battling settler colonialism is no walk in the park. It came with its fair share of challenges, setbacks, and hurdles. From discriminatory employment practices to disparaging beauty standards, colonialism cast a long shadow that Black women had to navigate and rise above.

Forging ahead with a sense of humor and sarcasm and persistently wagging their fingers at this Eurocentric nuisance, Black women crafted new narratives that didn't garner a stamp of approval from the colonial status quo. Who needs support when you've got the resilience and unmatched wisdom of generations to back you up?

So, even though settler colonialism seems to never want to take the hint that its presence is unwelcome, Black women have stood tall, drawing from their deep ancestral roots and tireless spirit to fight for their place and cultural integrity all day, every day.

In this stubborn tussle with settler colonialism, Black women emerged as tenacious warriors, persisting amidst adversity and navigating through choppy waters with strength and grace. Sure, they might still send the occasional sarcastic postcard to the Eurocentric hegemony, but ultimately, they've carved their own path, rooted in a rich heritage that refuses to be silenced.

If you ever need a dose of inspiration to tackle life, look no further than the unwavering resilience of Black women in their fight against settler colonialism. Because if they can stand up against centuries of Eurocentric garbage, what's stopping the rest of us?

Interplay of Gender and Social Constructs

The intersection of gender and social constructs is ground zero, where Black women put up a good fight, not just against settler colonialism but also against a patriarchal system fraught with bias. Black women have been clashing with the mongoose called patriarchy since, well, time started ticking. The ole chap believes in a flippant norm that puts men atop the pyramid, leaving women to scamper about its bottom. What fun! But Black women don't cut a deal with this narrative. No, they've been wrestling with this norm, tackling the stronger sex's "superiority" claim.

Let's back this up with more than just sass. Women warriors like Rosa Parks and Maya Angelou were not just challenging racial hegemony; they were outright defying gender stereotypes, flipping the domineering patriarchy into a well-deserved bird. Hell yes, they did! They were challenging not just the 'set rule' by settlers but also confronting beliefs ingrained deeply in society.

Alright, moving on to the even more stimulating part—breaking free from the 'inferior' mold—Black women do not just shatter the glass ceiling; they rocket past it, and if they could get a word to the grand old patriarchy down below, it would be, "Eat my stardust!"

Jokes aside, breaking free doesn't mean they transform overnight into these fierce avatars. Breaking free meant embracing who they were and boldly asserting their worth in the world. Some may consider the Black woman's body a symbol of inferiority and subjugation. But ha! Think again. They have turned their bodies into arenas of celebration, proudly displaying their cultural heritage through hairstyles, tattoos, and shades of melanin.

It's a mold-breaker of a paradox, isn't it? At one end, they are expected to remain confined by their skin color; at the other, they liberate themselves by their skin color. It's like society said, "Fit in this tiny box of inferiority," and Black women went, "Honey, I'm going to need a bigger box."

This is not a Discovery Channel feature on Black women; this is just a smidgen of their reality. They aren't falling in line with society's tedious norms or the colonial tags of inferiority. They are redefining their path, forging an intrinsically powerful, unexpectedly vibrant, and historically transformative way. Daring to confront the system, Black women surely know how to show patriarchal ideals at the exit door.

Modern Challenges Facing Black Women

In the modern world, issues such as racial and gender disparity are relics of the past, right? If only that was the case! Today, we'll be diving headfirst into the challenges that our resilient Black women face in this perfectly imperfect world where unicorns exist and the fight for equity is a fabled legend.

In our modern utopia, Black women, shockingly, continue to encounter racial and gender disparities. Whether it's the gaping wage gap or the devastating lack of representation in positions of power, Black women have the oh-so-exciting challenge of battling both racism and sexism. Why stick to tackling just one form of discrimination when you can ambitiously take on two?

Black women also get to participate in the fierce competition of beauty standards, where Eurocentric features reign supreme despite, you know, the existence of diverse features across the globe. Standing on the sidelines, those with distinctively African features must wonder, "Where did this memo come from?" It's almost like someone, somewhere, had a hidden agenda to keep an entire group of people feeling inadequate.

Alas, the struggle for equity is on. Black women are not only fighting for a fair playing field; they're building their own playing fields. With everything in place—terminator-style determination, an undying belief in justice, and just a pinch of sarcasm—they are tearing down oppressive structures, brick by brick.

In good old Herculean fashion, Black women juggle various roles, such as mothers, breadwinners, and activists, just to name a few. Functioning as an octopus might be helpful, but who needs eight arms when you've got the strength and resilience that Black women possess? Your role model, Hercules, might have superhuman strength, but can he compete with the relentless spirit of these warriors? I didn't think so.

Educating themselves to navigate the many minefields of a world not initially built for their success, Black women move forward with confidence. They cultivate spaces where their voices are heard, their stories are told, and their resilience is celebrated. Make way, society, because these trailblazers are refusing to back down.

Imagine a future where Black women don't have to face this double whammy of racism and sexism. A future where they can exhibit their talents and abilities without being hindered by the ever-present boogeyman of discrimination. Doesn't that just sound magical? Hold onto your hats because, with the relentless spirit of Black women, that magical future is closer than ever.

So, here's to Black women: tirelessly navigating the treacherous waters of racial and gender disparities, boldly charting a course towards equity, and proving time and time again that resilience is encoded in their very genes.

Paying Tribute to Resilient Black Women

Women measure life not by the number of breaths they take but by the staggering moments that leave them breathless. That's resilience. They're the backbone of their communities, the tenacity personified, the absolute personification of strength. They're deep-rooted trees swaying, but not breaking, in the storm—not just weathering it, but using it to grow, aiming for the sky, touching the stars while their roots remain firmly grounded. And, might I add, doing it all while keeping their hair flawless? Can we get an "amen" in here?

Now, let's pen an ode to these warriors. These women are the guiding northern stars, from Rosa Parks to Michelle Obama and from Beyonce to Amanda Gorman. They rose from the shackles of a system designed to suppress them, broke free from the centuries-old yoke, and smashed every glass ceiling on their way up. They are warriors in every sense of the word, and let no one tell you otherwise.

So, let's lift our glasses for these inspirational demi-goddesses who persist and resist, succeeding against all odds. A toast to the Afro-futuristic warriors, the real-life superheroes who don't need capes. More power to you, ladies. Keep those heels high and your standards higher.

CHAPTER 3: NURTURING FORTITUDE: UNRAVELING THE MATERNAL ROLES AND SOCIETAL PRESSURES OF BLACK WOMEN'S MOTHERHOOD AS A SOURCE OF STRENGTH

African American women have this undeniable, extraordinary strength that makes you wonder how they manage to pull off everyday life without losing their marbles. That very strength has allowed them to play numerous influential roles in society, whether as mothers, daughters, sisters, or social workers. But with great power comes great responsibility, and these incredible beings are no exception to the rule.

Now, let's talk about some of the societal pressures resting on their mighty shoulders, shall we? Racism? Check. Sexism? Check. Racial loyalty and oppression? Absolutely. But instead of letting these adversities weigh them down, African American women have turned them into a source of strength. In their infinite wisdom, they've managed to channel these experiences into something incredibly empowering.

We can't possibly discuss their epic fortitude without mentioning their innate ability to play the roles of both mother and social worker. Just imagine the relentless whirlwind that is in their lives—cooking, cleaning, nurturing, counseling, advocating, breathing (bless them for remembering to breathe!)—all while wearing a perpetual smile on their faces. And if that's somehow not enough, they're also burdened with a myriad of internal conflicts, like the strong Black woman stereotype, imposter syndrome, and the superwoman schema. Talk about having your work cut out for you!

So, where does one find solace amidst this cruel and relentless storm? By balancing it out with a decent measure of support systems, self-care, and a good old dose of advocacy for societal change, because one thing's for sure: if anyone deserves to sit back, relax, and just take a moment for themselves, it's these women.

And at the heart of it all, this journey celebrates African American mothers' sheer resilience and fortitude. It's high time we break down those pesky stereotypes, shift societal narratives, and honor the awe-inspiring contributions that these women have made to our world.

Historical Context

Picture yourself in 1619, when African American women were thrown headfirst into forced servitude. No consent, no choice—just trying to stay afloat amidst the tumultuous sea of life. But wait! Do you hear that? It's the sound of resilience chugging through adversity. The beautiful symphony of survival, sung by these steppingstones of society, resonates through the annals of history.

As we speed into the future, slow down a bit. Here, in today's world, we see a drastically different image. African American women now possess personal and professional choices. Good riddance to bad rubbish. It's about time! Alongside their role as mothers, many have chosen the noble path of being social workers. Talk about wearing multiple hats! The kitchen apron on one hand and the superhero cape on the other—it's like a sartorial paradox. They have bravely stepped into the shoes of nurturers and providers, building a rampart against societal pressures.

But how did this shift happen, you ask? Look no further than historical events that played the unspoken role of the puppet master pulling the strings. Hello, gender roles! Good day, wars! Salutations, civil rights movement! All of these, among others, have deeply impacted the essence of motherhood among African American women.

However, history is like the in-laws—important, but far from perfect (Oh, you thought I was going to be only sappy and respectful, didn't you?). Like a boomerang, history has thrown back some complicated repercussions—a delectable cocktail of progress and setbacks. Remember, when life gives you lemons, make lemonade, but don't forget to watch out for the seeds!

I've noticed a fascinating trend: we often talk about history like we've graduated from a Time Travel 101 course. "Back in my day, things were so much different." Didn't those living through those moments think the same about their past? The cycle loops, the soap opera of time continues, and voila! Here we are, where motherhood among African American women is a complex mosaic woven with threads of resilience, tenacity, struggles, and societal pressures—the past echoes in every decision, every nurturing act, and every moment of fortitude.

History is not just a dusty old museum exhibit. It's a living, breathing entity, adapting with time, and shaping the present. It feeds into the power of choice that African American women now have while simultaneously influencing their ongoing pressures. And trust me, no matter what century we're in, managing societal expectations while raising human beings is equivalent to tightrope walking on a telephone wire. Bravery or insanity? You decide!

As we travel back to today, let's not forget that these women not only juggle motherhood and their jobs but also grapple with an exhausting array of historical imprints. Yet, despite history's rollercoaster ride, one thing stands constant: the unwavering strength of African American mothers.

The Dual Roles of Mother and Social Worker

Hold on to your hats, folks, because if you thought being a mother was a full-time job, wait until you hear about the double whammy that African American women face as mothers and social workers. Why settle for just one superhero cape when you can wear two? Am I right? But do these superwomen ever have to deal with the evils of role overload, strain, and confusion that come with juggling multiple identities?

Role overload and time management:

There is no need to rub your eyes; we genuinely mentioned balancing motherhood and social work. Can you imagine scheduling playdates while advocating for your clients? It's a real juggling act. African American women have been multitasking before it became a buzzword. But, as amazing as these women are, the struggle with managing time and feeling overloaded is real. A mere 24 hours a day? They could use some extra hours, like those pizza coupons they keep forgetting to use. Instead, African American mothers in social work often find themselves catching up on their favorite reality TV shows (or sleeping) at 3 a.m. because, hey, a woman's gotta do what a woman's gotta do.

Role strain and emotional demands:

When you're a superwoman, you might think emotional demands are like dust particles—you just brush them off. But even the strongest of all superheroes need to recharge their batteries. The emotional strain of dealing with work-related issues while managing personal responsibilities can stretch a person to their limit. As if managing children's tantrums and teen drama wasn't enough, try balancing the challenges faced by clients in social work. It's like never shutting down your laptop because you simply can't escape the work emails (and trust us, they never end). The emotional support blankets and occasional venting sessions are practically non-negotiable necessities to maintain that remarkable strength.

Role confusion and Self-identity:

Mother? Social worker? Wonder Woman? Keeping track of these African American women's ever-changing roles can be tough. However, self-identity is crucial for mental and emotional well-being. It's tricky to navigate the various positions and expectations that society thrusts upon them, like unwanted flyers on a busy street. Is she the nurturer? The advocate? The protector? The cheerleader? Yes, to all, but finding the balance in these numerous roles can sometimes feel like taking a stroll on a tightrope while chewing gum, texting, and drinking coffee. It's not the easiest task, but these women are amazing.

In a nutshell, our superhero African American women, who juggle being mothers and social workers, face a multitude of challenges. Their ability to manage time, handle emotional demands, and maintain their sense of identity while fighting off the bad guys (AKA societal pressures) is beyond admirable. So, here's to celebrating these phenomenal women who continue to make the world a better place. Let's make sure we lend them our support, our ears, and maybe, occasionally, our shoulder to lean on, because even superheroes need a little help sometimes.

Societal Challenges

Who said handling societal challenges was a cakewalk? Certainly not for the mighty African American women who gracefully oversee the dual roles of being a mother and a social worker while dealing with racism, sexism, racial loyalty, and gender biases. It's like ordering a double cheeseburger with a side of societal pressure.

Let's begin with the most unwanted toppings: racism and sexism. Sadly, these two flavors just won't go away! For African American women, a day without encountering racist or sexist remarks may feel as rare as a perfectly ripe avocado. They face the "double jeopardy" of being discriminated against for their race and gender, often experiencing verbal attacks, microaggressions, and belittling comments. And yet, they rise above all, like Beyoncé conquering the music industry. Who runs the world? Girls!

Moving on to another not-so-tasty ingredient, we have the delightful "racial loyalty and oppression" combo. The long-standing history of oppression and racial inequality has pressured African American women into putting their community's needs before their own. It's like saying, "No, I'll just have the leftover veggies." You take the juicy steak." Black women carry the burden of lifting their people while simultaneously battling systemic racism and inequality. They're like the superheroes every community could use, but nobody wants to acknowledge them.

Finally, let's talk about those stale croutons we find sprinkled all over: gender biases and discrimination. As moms and social workers, African American women are expected to uphold traditional gender roles and be the primary caregivers for their children, even in households with two working parents. Are we still living in the 1950s? Whether it's in the workplace or at home, they face constant discrimination and stereotypes; it's as if gender biases are the gum stuck to the bottom of their shoe, gross but hard to get rid of. No one should put up with this, not even strong women like Oprah or Michelle Obama.

Despite these less-than-appetizing circumstances, African American women continue to strut their stuff and make the world better. Aren't they basically the WD-40 of society, fixing and lubricating all the rusty parts? They constantly face and overcome these societal challenges, and it's about time we started recognizing their resilience and power. Go Queens!

Before we wrap up this flavorful discussion, let's remind ourselves that managing societal challenges is no easy task. Yet, African American women manage to do all this while being the primary caregivers for their families, just like the most delicious pizza with all the right toppings. What's their secret recipe? We may never know, but one thing is for sure: no amount of societal challenges can keep these incredible women down.

Next time you see an African American woman juggling her many roles and overcoming these challenges, make sure to give her the respect and praise she deserves. They've earned their right to be celebrated, and we look forward to seeing more positive change in the world as they continue leading the way. After all, what's a better tribute to Black women than recognizing their grit and resilience?

Internal Conflicts

The complexities we weave when we're trying so hard to achieve. Being a Black woman in our world is no walk in the park. And no, I'm not talking about finding matching shoes for that killer dress. So, let's talk serious business, shall we? Buckle up, folks!

First off, we have this not-so-fabulous thing called the 'strong Black woman' stereotype. Ever come across the phrase, "Black women are supposed to endure all things, conquer all things, and never feel pain"? Yes, that's the one! It's like having an annoying mosquito buzzing in your ear 24/7, reminding you, no pressure, but you superhuman or bust, honey! It's like being the female version of Hercules, minus that epic soundtrack. And let's face it, there's no one-size-fits-all in human nature, so why should it be any different for Black women?

Can we please talk about that irritating bloke called the Imposter Syndrome? That little voice in your head constantly whispers, "Do you really belong here?" "Are you good enough?" Imagine trying to win a marathon while your shoelaces are constantly getting untied. It's even more frustrating when you're killing it in your career, climbing the success ladder, breaking those glass ceilings, and bam! This uninvited, unwelcome guest, AKA self-doubt, crashes the party.

Lastly, welcome to the world of the Superwoman schema! It sounds awesome, right? We are like stars in the comic book universe. The only downside? This universe conveniently forgets the existence of kryptonite. The unspoken societal expectation of being a perfect mom, an unwavering professional, a flawless homemaker, a caring daughter, wife, sister, you name it, takes a toll. It's like Black women are expected to be juggling chainsaws while riding a unicycle. On a tightrope. Over a shark tank. Still, considering the sass, the class, and the brass Black women are made of, it is no surprise they even sometimes manage to pull that off.

Now, amidst all these mental Olympics, where does this leave our African American ladies? A crossroad where they master that headstand to defy gravity or indulge in some serious reality checks to take off the extra weight. As my grandma used to say, Black doesn't crack, but it does creak sometimes when these stereotypes pile up! It's nothing a righteous sit-down, global reality check, and a couple of rounds of spirited conversation can't handle.

Now that we've straightened out a few crinkles, let's hear it one more time for every Black woman out there: you don't have anything to prove to anyone. You just keep doing you!

Strengths and Gaps in Existing Theories

Who doesn't love a good theoretical framework to help us make sense of the world? In African American mothers' cases, some theories help us understand their experiences of strength and motherhood. However, existing theories aren't perfect—we still need a comprehensive theory covering all the bases.

Exploring the links between strength and mental health is another fascinating area. It might seem counterintuitive to some, but being an all-powerful, unbreakable superwoman is not so great for mental health. It turns out that carrying the weight of the world isn't easy on anyone. Who knew? More seriously, the pressure to be strong can result in selflessness, powerlessness, and self-silencing, which can contribute to psychological distress and mental health issues. Building on this, it's important that we appreciate how the concept of strength can both support and challenge African American mothers.

So, where do we go from here? If only we had a comprehensive theory to make it all make sense. Oh, wait, that's what we're asking for here! An approach that takes into account the nuances of race, gender, motherhood, and professional identities for African American women who happen to be both mothers and social workers would kind of be the holy grail in this situation.

Picture a theory that accounts for historical context, societal pressures, internal conflicts, and existing theories' strengths and weaknesses. Maybe it could even throw in the secret recipe for the perfect chocolate cake (although that might be asking for too much). However, developing a more comprehensive theory that incorporates all the factors we've discussed would be a true achievement.

Of course, producing this theory won't be a walk in the park. It requires research, dialogue, and critical thinking (you know, the fun stuff). But it's an essential step in understanding the experiences of African American mothers who bravely navigate multiple competing roles and societal pressures.

In the meantime, let's not forget to salute these women's resilience, grit, and sheer awesomeness. They're forging ahead in challenging circumstances and creating a better world for the next generation by standing firm against injustice and inequality. So, here's to the African American mothers who kick butt every day and deserve a comprehensive theory that truly recognizes the complexity of their lives.

And remember, it's not just about having the right theoretical framework; it's about making sure that it doesn't gather dust on a shelf. With the right theory in hand, we can forge ahead in empowering African American mothers, creating awareness, and finally challenging the narratives that have held these strong women back for far too long.

Potential Solutions and Strategies

Picture your everyday superwoman soaring high in the sky, but there's an invisible parachute strapped to her back, her friends, her family, and a network of other superwomen.

Often, it's much easier to tackle your demons when you're not the only one wrestling with them. The 'strong Black woman' stereotype can be a heavy mantle to bear. Still, with collective care, solidarity, understanding, and humor (yes, plenty of that because nothing diffuses tension faster than a good laugh), these pressures can be, if not breezed through, at least eased.

Self-care might sound like an overused buzzword, but it's as essential as oxygen to fire when applied to our superwomen. While self-neglect might earn some temporary validation through applause for "strength," it's as dangerous as having kryptonite in Superman's breakfast cereal. Just as you can't pour from an empty cup, you can't juggle chainsaws without risking a severed limb or two. If African

American mothers are to sustain their nurturing, they must factor in moments of rest, rejuvenation, and maybe a day to just not care about the world's to-do list.

Mental health is not a luxury; it's as basic as your morning espresso. Give these women the space to vent, express their anxieties and fears, and lend an ear when they want to discuss them. It might just save them from the brink of mental exhaustion.

Having established the support and self-care systems, it's time to address the elephant in the room: societal ignorance. Hey, don't groan. It's faster than waiting for evolution to kick in. More light must be shed on these superwomen's professional and personal struggles; advocacy for change is imperative.

Remember, even Superman needed Lois Lane to tell his story? Sharing stories, facts, and experiences of African American mothers can initiate conversations, and God willing, if the conversers have two brain cells to rub together, changes in attitudes, policies, and social norms can occur.

Raising awareness can change the 'strong Black woman' narrative to 'strong because of support, self-care, and societal awareness.' After all, even superheroes have a trusty Alfred in their lives.

So, as we navigate the gauntlet of applause, adventures, and adversities, let's raise a toast to our superwomen, unburden their capes, and give them the recognition they deserve—not as symbols of relentless strength but as humans with vulnerabilities, capable of unmeasurable resilience when wrapped in understanding and compassion. And perhaps then, they might just have a moment to kick off their boots, unwind that cape, and relish that deep sigh of relief they've been holding onto for so long.

In the end, as the saying goes, 'Many hands make light work,' even if we're talking about the formidable African American mothers! Their contributions need to be celebrated with more than just a zip-lip tribute but a proactive pledge to ensure their empowerment! Now, isn't that worth a resounding 'hell yeah!'

Celebrating the Resilience and Fortitude of African American Mothers

The resilience and fortitude of African American mothers is a topic we simply can't ignore. So, gather around kids; it's time to break down some stereotypes, shift societal narratives, and honor these amazing women's contributions. Are you ready for this rollercoaster ride?

First up, breaking down stereotypes—because, let's face it, stereotypes are as inescapable as a half-empty jar of Nutella in a house full of hungry kids. But wait, scratch that—they don't have to be. It's often assumed that African American women are somehow expected to juggle ten bowling balls while wearing six-inch heels. News flash: they're not mythical superheroes. They are just as human as you and me, with their own unique strengths and challenges.

You may think you've gathered the courage for a quick juice break. Not so fast, honey! It's time to jump into the next fascinating point: shifting societal narratives. Yes, that's right. The stories we tell ourselves matter, as dictated by Oprah, Dr. Phil, and pretty much any wise TED Talk speaker. We've got to flip the narrative on its head and embrace the value of the multicultural motherhood experience. Different backgrounds and perspectives bring innovation and wisdom to the table, and that's something worth celebrating. Plus, think about the incredible potlucks this cultural mix would produce.

We've celebrated resilience and grit, but now it's time to toast the incredible contributions of African American mothers. From civil rights icons to political leaders and artists, these phenomenal women have left an indelible mark on history and our hearts. So, let's raise a glass to their achievements and remember that their legacies are our collective responsibility to protect and cherish.

Now, let's forge ahead and continue celebrating the incredible journey of African American mothers everywhere. Let's not just pay lip service but truly take action to recognize and honor their resilience and fortitude in all aspects of society. Because, you know, it's only fair.

Understanding the maternal roles of African American women isn't just a 'nice-to-have'; it's a 'need-to-have.' Why? Because busting myths and switching narratives always is. We've been shouting from the rooftops about this, and let's keep doing just that. After all, empowering these mothers paves the way for a better, brighter, and more equitable future.

CHAPTER 4: EMBRACING RESILIENCE: THE SPIRITUAL AND EMOTIONAL FORTITUDE OF BLACK WOMEN THROUGH FAITH AND INNER STRENGTH

Once upon a time, in a world not too far from ours, there lived an extraordinary demographic of women known as "Black women." Now, these women aren't your regular Jill or Jane. They are the epitome of resilience, colorful personalities, and believe it or not, some serious 'can do' attitude.

Black women are not forged from the ordinary and are often associated with an image of strength, resilience, and an unwavering spirit. They scatter gold dust on the path wherever they go, catching everyone's attention with their sheer presence. This power isn't the result of some magic potion. It was developed over years of struggles, frosty life experiences, and the continual battle of being both a woman and a Black woman. The combo can make the bravest of hearts quake, I tell you.

Now, let's shine a spotlight on their emotional and spiritual strength. You must be thinking, "What? They get spiritual, too." Absolutely! Never underestimate a Black woman juggling life's lemons and making lemonade while simultaneously meditating on her favorite Bible and Quran verses. Any guesses for the secret sauce? It's faith! Faith is stronger than any knight's armor—faith that dares to see a silver lining in the storm's epicenter.

Black women's life stories are filled with instances where faith tackled life's bulldozers. Their faith isn't merely solace but a robust defense mechanism and pretty much their cheerleading squad. It's as if faith whispers into their ear, "You go, girl!" Hands down, faith takes center stage in the grand spectacle of their lives.

Pardon me, but if you ever come across someone denying the emotional strength of Black women, send them my way. I'll set them straight! These women are rock solid, like LEGO structures glued together. Except their glue isn't childish fantasies, but a blend of emotional resilience stirred with a hefty dose of spirituality.

Harnessing Strength Through Faith: Navigating the Waters of Life

Yes, we're talking about the divine GPS that has guided many Black women through the tumultuous storms of life. They say when the going gets tough, the tough get going. But wait, let's add a twist to that. When the going gets tough, the authoritarian turns to faith.

Picture this: there's chaos all around—life can be a bitter old hag, throwing lemons left, right, and center (not even the cocktail kind!). Right then, with a grace and dignity that can put a ballet dancer to shame, a Black woman steps up and says, "Bring it on!" And who do you think is her secret weapon? It's that rock-solid faith—her ever-faithful anchor in turbulent times.

Well, things have certainly gotten interesting here. I love a good story, don't you? Well, I've got a stash right here for your late-night story cravings, bubbling over with tales of faith-providing fortitude. Remember the little old lady gingerly crossing the road, her faith steadier than her stick? Or that woman who braved the tempestuous sea of heartbreak, loss, and disappointment, rowing on the oars of her unwavering faith? Yes, me neither! But these stories left an impression, right? These aren't your regular fairy tales. Nope, these are anthems of resilience, stinging slaps on life's face, singing, "We won't go down, not today, not any day!"

Do you remember that quote? Yes, that one says, "I can do all things through Christ who strengthens me." Don't you wonder who said it? Was it Nelson Mandela during his incarceration, or maybe Harriet Tubman during those audacious escape orchestras? Wrong on both counts. Close your jaws, folks; these were the resolute words of our very own Black women. Tagging onto their faith and exploring spirituality, they've breathed life into these words, turning pressures into perseverance. Every Black woman is a sparkling mirror, reflecting strength and fortitude.

Remember, when you think you've hit rock bottom, there is always faith. After all, diamonds take form under pressure, and every Black woman is indeed a rare and precious diamond! Embrace the rollercoaster, for the thrill is in riding the highs and the lows. And who knows? Perhaps the view at the bottom is as breathtaking as the one from the top. To life, to faith, to a strength unknown!

Unleashing the Superwoman: Embracing Uncommon Strength in Common Challenges

When we think of superheroes, we often envision folks in spandex with capes fluttering in the wind while they fight evil and bring justice.

Superwoman Ethos is not about being able to fly or lift heavy objects (though the ability to juggle multiple tasks at once is no less heroic if you ask us). Instead, it's about the indomitable spirit and strength that Black women channel in their everyday lives to overcome the seemingly insurmountable challenges they face.

Here's the real double-scoop sundae for you, though: while being a Black woman in a society biased towards gender and race might sound like double jeopardy, it only breeds double strength. When you have to deal with two scoops of difficulties, you get twice as much resilience in return; that's how life likes to balance its books.

But guess what? Being a superwoman doesn't mean that they don't hit potholes on this journey. They face societal obstacles, but the fun part is that they don't just survive; they thrive. For instance, picture that corporate ladder, shiny but riddled with unseen barriers. Our superwomen don't just climb; they pole-vault over it.

Now, assume you're in a room. The room has four walls, right? However, let's peg them as obstacles—prejudice, disparity, stereotyping, and bias. You want to get out, so what do you do? Knock one down. Too simple. Black women constantly defy these societal "rooms" by building doors and windows, essentially creating their own exits.

Picture them in a society that deals constant blows—they're like those inflatable bozo punching bags. Push them, punch them, and they'll fall, but they bounce back every single time.

However, these societal obstacles aren't like an obstacle course on some reality show. This is the real world, where the stakes are high and the challenges are personal, with no cheesy background music.

And yet, they continue to demonstrate how to rise above it—how to smile in the face of adversity and turn every setback into a setup for a comeback. They know precisely how to play the cards they've been dealt, even when they've got a hand that would make any poker player cry.

So, let's not classify our Superwomen as mere fighters; they are survivors, warriors, and champions who carry the world on their shoulders and manage to do it with grace and style.

From fighting the pay gap and smashing glass ceilings to battling discrimination, they never cease to amaze us with their grit. And yes, while spiders and heights might give some of them the heebie-jeebies (who're we kidding, it scares the daylight out of us, too), they never shy away from the bigger battles.

But let's ditch the seriousness here for a moment and appreciate the fun side of this. Imagine being able to say, "I fought prejudice at work; what did you do today?" during a casual dinner conversation. Talk about an exciting day!

A day in the life of a Black woman—slaying it every step of the way.

Preserving Self and Family: The Indomitable Spirit of Black Women

The indomitably spirited Black women somehow maneuver the art of surviving through life's adversities while clutching firmly to their dignity like a prized possession. Their modus operandi? Ah! Here is the heartwarming, comforting cradle of family. It's as if they've evolved to strengthen their bones with a touch of titanium, resilient and unbending in the face of adversity.

Picture a seasoned sailor, undeterred by the angry storm, gracefully gliding her ship over the rolling waves. That is the Black woman's expertise in steering the familial ship and maintaining equilibrium despite the forces threatening disruption.

You'd think a lady's got to clock in the beauty sleep, right? Nope! Their sacrifice knows no bounds! If you ever wonder what keeps them from hitting the snooze button, the answer lies in a potent determination that remains unmatched. They are driven by the audacious dream of crafting their children into 'better people'; phew, talk about shooting for the stars!

Their children grow up fed on a steady diet of resilience, determination, and self-worth, a recipe that churns out the unshakable fortitude seen stamped on every Black woman. They aren't just breeding the next generation; they are architecting a lineage of strength and superwomen.

But let's not get too carried away. After all, they aren't exactly manufacturing "better people" in a hidden backyard workshop. And sure as hell, they aren't being stamped 'strong' on some god-forsaken assembly line. This strength is born from the fires of adversity and nurtured in the soil by an unyielding spirit.

For these women, self-preservation is a combination of art and sport, not to mention drama and sitcoms. It's about surviving the wild storms with grace, or, as they put it, "riding the bull without messing up the hairdo."

But in the grand theater of life, nothing is handed on a silver platter. Preserving oneself and one's family often comes at the great price of personal sacrifices, long sleepless nights, and a relentless will to strive. It's like engaging in a never-ending wrestling match with life and emerging as the victor every single time.

The beauty is that they don't do it for applause, recognition, or even a thank-you note. They do it, quite simply, for love. The propagation of the Black woman's strength is a love story, complete with its dramatic episodes. Full of tearjerker moments, hearty laughs, painful silences, and a heck of a climax, these are real-life superheroes with superpowers grounded in love and sheer perseverance.

It's not just about the survival of Black women. It's about the survival of a dream—a dream of a better future, a stronger family, and a resilient community.

Empowerment Through Education and Community Engagement

After understanding the formidable journey of Black women through faith and struggles, let's turn a page and explore the beacon of hope that education plays in their relentless pursuit of resilience. Education is not just a catalyst but also the alchemist that transforms the base metal of struggle into the gold of empowerment and strength. It's almost like an interactive fairytale that comes with a "terms and conditions" clause. The term is "hard work," and the condition is "persistence."

Our phenomenal ladies do not shy away from these. Instead, they stomp high with their steel-toed boots of perseverance and resilience, climbing the education ladder, each rung echoing with triumphant laughter in the face of adversity. The brighter the light of knowledge, the bolder the silhouettes of power and self-reliance—all thanks to education.

Shifting gears, let's glide into the role of community involvement. This isn't your regular hands-on Potluck Planning Committee; we're talking about involvement that delightfully forces the needle to stitch resilience into the societal fabric. The Black woman doesn't just involve herself in the community; she is the community.

Imagine her as a beautiful patchwork quilt, with each patch telling a different story of struggle, survival, strength, and success. She doesn't just cover; she emboldens, endowing everyone around her with the warmth of her spirit. It's love and strength in action, ladies and gentlemen, transforming neighborhoods into fortresses of unwavering solidarity.

Now, embrace yourself because we're about to discuss a phenomenon that runs deep, generation after generation—the passing of resilience from one woman to another. In these quiet, intimate moments, resilience is successfully transferred, like a precious family heirloom, wrapped in stories of old, telling tales of strength, courage, and willpower.

It's like an unspoken tradition, kind of like how Aunt Maureen always brings her infamous potato salad to family reunions—only that instead of questionable potato salad, these women bring stories of endurance that inspire and teach the future generations to stand tall, to be unbroken, and to embrace the glorious resilience that runs in their veins.

These exchanges make them not just resilience carriers but resilience heroes, the "supe-her-woman," an avatar much more engaging and captivating than any comic book superhero wannabe can ever aspire to be!

So, as we sail through the ocean of Black women's resilience, it's worth noting that the winds of change are stirred by education, loaded with community involvement, and driven by generational wisdom. It's a powerful amalgamation, isn't it? Irony called, and it's laughing at the stark comparison between this powerhouse of strength and Aunt Maureen's potato salad!

If our amazing women can imbibe such strong resilience from generations of hardship and triumph, imagine the avalanche of change we'd witness if these empowered women were given the right opportunities and the acknowledgment they deserve!

Unmasking the Strong Black Woman: Understanding the Hidden Costs

It's all very inspiring until you realize that not even superheroes keep their capes on 24/7. While we're all applauding the marathon runner, perhaps it's important to remember: she's the one huffing and puffing and wishing somebody would serve up some lemonade at the finish line.

So, let's peek under the proverbial mask and meet the real woman, daring to be herself, despite the monumental expectations sent skyrocketing by societal norms. The woman who, just like the rest of us, sometimes struggles to get out of bed on rainy Monday mornings (and Tuesday, Wednesday, you get the picture). The woman who, while appearing to juggle career, family, and community obligations like a Cirque du Soleil performer, often lies awake at night worrying how she'll pull off the next big performance.

Being a Superwoman doesn't mean you don't feel pain; it just means you've been attending the School of Acting Tough for so long that the admission notice for the School of Sane Living got lost in the post. And here's the punchline, folks: not every damsel is in distress, but every damsel does feel pain. See the difference?

Embrace the T word. You know, the one we hate to admit: vulnerability. After all, Pepé Le Pew learned the hard way that constant pursuit without a breather only leads to exhaustion and being shooed away with a broom (and I'm sure he's seen the inside of many a skunk therapist's office). If vulnerability means embracing the fact that you're a human with real emotions, then it's high time everyone got a bit more touchy-feely.

That said, let's not forget that, just like everyone else, many Black women live in the broad daylight of diverse mental health challenges. What? You thought that cape was bulletproof? Reality check: even Superwoman gets days off. Yet many Black women are busy saving the world when they should be writing in their mood journals or attending well-organized, comfortable group therapy sessions with free doughnuts and coffee. Because sisters, strength, and resilience are great, but no one can always live up to the unyielding Superwoman trope—it's too darn heavy a title to carry.

In celebration of the real super sheroes—those who dare to say that when the going gets tough, the tough also needs nap time—let's remember that resilience and faith aren't just about fighting. They're also about resting, reflecting, and understanding that taking off that cape is okay sometimes.

Towards a Brighter Future: Transforming Challenges into Opportunities

The future is the shiny, elusive concept that always seems just around the corner, wouldn't you agree? For the incredible and resilient Black women in our lives, there are challenges to conquer and opportunities to seize with open arms. Now, let's dive headfirst into the murky waters of gender, race, and depression!

If you've ever had one of those days where you feel like the whole world is against you, imagine carrying that weight while being burdened with prejudices and stereotypes simply because you're a Black woman. I mean, come on, people, it's the 21st century! It's high time we shed some light on the challenges ahead and break down these prejudiced barriers! Exposing and addressing mental health disparities faced by Black women is long overdue and essential to reshaping that brighter future we all so crave for them.

"Hey there, supportive structures, where have you been hiding?" Well, pleasantries aside, society must embrace and cultivate an environment where Black women have access to mental health care, resources, and safe spaces. Yes, it's 20-whatever, and it's finally time for everyone to pitch in so these strong, resilient Black women, who have been carrying the world on their shoulders for far too long, can have a well-deserved break.

In a world where Black women still face prejudice and discrimination, it's essential to create equal opportunities, provide appropriate education, and promote an inclusive society that values the contributions of these amazing women.

And now, for the grand finale: the role of supportive structures! From churches and community organizations to family and friends, many support structures influence the resilience and strength of Black women. While it's true that everyone faces challenges in life, the power of resilience found in Black women is unmatched. So, let's all take a moment to cheer on this fierce determination and unwavering faith deeply ingrained in Black women's spirits, minds, and souls everywhere.

In this journey towards a brighter future, it's essential to recognize, celebrate, and embrace Black women's courage, determination, and spiritual fortitude. These amazing individuals have shown us all that greatness can be achieved even in the harshest of environments. And who knows, maybe if we all take a page from their resilience book, we'll be ready to tackle life's obstacles alongside these phenomenal women, discovering new opportunities and chances for personal growth. So, for what are we waiting? Let's keep the legacy of their strength alive and support these incredible women on their path toward personal development and a more equitable future.

CHAPTER 5: UNITY IN DIVERSITY: EMBRACING INTERSECTIONALITY FOR COLLECTIVE PROGRESS – A PERSPECTIVE ON BLACK WOMEN'S EXPERIENCES

You see, intersectionality isn't just a ten-dollar word university students use to sound smart. It's a living, breathing, and ever-evolving concept that helps us see how different identities (like race, gender, or economic status) intersect to shape our life experiences. Imagine yourself standing at the epicenter of a web, each strand representing different parts of your identity, like being a Black woman or a Latina, being bisexual, or being economically disadvantaged. All these strands come together and form your uniquely beautiful yet complex reality.

Embracing intersectionality isn't about playing "Identity Olympics." No, darling, it's about recognizing our shared struggle against diverse forms of oppression and forging forward collectively. It's like becoming a human version of the Avengers, where each superhero joins forces to address the Thanos(es) of societal inequalities. How cool is that?

So, at this point, you might be wondering, "Why the laser focus on Black women's experiences?" Excellent question, and no, it's not because we've run out of Netflix shows to binge-watch. It's because being a Black woman brings its own unique set of challenges—a race-gender-double-bubble-trouble, if you will. Their experiences can offer us profound insights into the intricate dynamics of intersectionality.

As we delve into this exciting adventure, let me remind you that your seatbelts need to be fastened, trays stowed away, and brace yourselves because it's going to be a bumpy but enlightening ride. The journey of understanding Black women's experiences and the intersectionality of their identities takes us through turbulent storms and winds of change. But remember, though the night is dark and full of terror, the sun does rise.

And yes, just a friendly reminder: if you hear someone ask, "Are we there yet?" gently tell them, "Honey, the journey has just begun!" After all, understanding the enigma of intersectionality isn't a sprint; it's a marathon!

Experiencing Intersectionality: Black Women's Perspectives

Imagine this: it's like walking down the road, whistling a tune, but every few seconds, you're forced to juggle chainsaws, dodge banana peels, and leap over potholes. You are dealing with your gender, race, and socioeconomic status all at once. That's when intersectionality moonwalks into the conversation.

And who would be better to cast as our protagonist for this episode than Quintessentially Powerful and Inspiring? Yes, you guessed it—Black women! It's no secret that life tosses them a Molotov cocktail of unique challenges wrapped up in sparkly paper called systemic discrimination.

We're not just referring to standing up against the odds, but dealing with the concerto of gender and race on a global orchestra stage. Amplified by the socioeconomic megaphone, it's a melody—one that many of us might find out of tune, but for them, it's just another Tuesday. Don't let the skin color fool you; Black is not just Black. It's nuanced, rich, diverse, and unforgivingly complex. They aren't just playing gender cards on the societal poker table; they are also tossing racial and economic ones, trying to form a winning hand.

But why let me do all the talking, eh? Let's hear some tales—not just any tales, but real spin-chilling, hair-raising stories straight from the trenches of the battlefield. Like a classic movie, we rewind to Rosa Parks, who might appear as just a "tired seamstress" refusing to give up her bus seat. Yet, this was a woman who kicked racism right where it hurt on a bus in Montgomery. Teresa, a 30-year-old single mother from the Bronx, shatters glass ceilings by day and moonlights for her online degree by night, defying all odds stacked against her.

Take a moment and think about Oprah, who's more than just a billionaire media mogul. She's a Black woman who survived poverty, abuse, and all the 'isms you can stack up, then educated, spun them around to give them a good ol' talk-show therapy! Now, that's what one calls bossing the game!

In the grand opera of life, where everyone's hustling their way through intermission, Black women are running the whole damn show—ticket counters, stage, spotlights—while juggling their personal lives offstage. You may ask, why are we frenzied about these stories? Well, it's about time we acknowledged the reality beyond our little bubbles.

So, as we raise the curtain on their stories, leaning into the discomfort is part of the process. Trust me, it's way more fun, like biting into a jalapeno, thinking it's a bell pepper, and getting that zing! Ah, the thrill of it!

Historical Movements and Black Women's Role

Picture, if you will, a time when the world was segregated in more ways than one. Then, enter the stage, our leads, the heroes of Black history. They did not politely knock on the door of change; oh no, they broke those barriers down and made sure they were welcomed.

Names like Rosa Parks—what a woman! Stuck in a world where racism was as regular as breathing, she proved that you didn't need to shout for your voice to be heard. Sometimes, all you need to do is sit still. Yes, she probably just wanted to sit still after a long day of work, but with that simple action, she beautifully punctuated the sentence of segregation.

Following closely in the path laid by her predecessors was Ruby Bridges. Oh, Ruby, what were you, six? And already being the face of resistance in the white-dominated education system! How many of us can say we changed the world before losing our baby teeth?

Our journey through history wouldn't be complete without a salute to The Women's Political Council (WPC), a band of Black women that might as well have been termed the 'Silent, but Deadly' species and known for tiptoeing under the radar yet executing the Montgomery Bus Boycott flawlessly!

Now, let's jump right into the present, where Michelle Obama has seamlessly transitioned from the corridors of the White House to an era dominated by social media trends. How she managed to do that while keeping her style so on point, we may never know! She's inspirational and a pioneer in her own right, encouraging young Black girls everywhere to question, stand tall, and dare to dream.

Cut to Oprah Winfrey, who, like a queen, reigns supreme over the media, creating a multi-billion-dollar empire out of sheer determination and a vision to educate and entertain. Her legacy leaves a tantalizing glimpse of what Black women are capable of when offered a level playing field.

And how could we leave out Tarana Burke, the quiet force behind the #MeToo movement? She made us all have those tough conversations about sexual harassment. Yes, they made us squirm, but boy, did they need to be had!

So, you see, historically, Black women haven't just been spectators; they've been catalysts, diligently and brilliantly chipping away at rigid societal norms to mold a more just and inclusive society. They've done it all with a sense of style and dynamism that's both audacious and legendary.

Nevertheless, while we're busy being starstruck by these trailblazers, let's not forget that they're a demonstration of the potential every Black woman holds. Day in and day out, Black women continue to shape society, their actions echoing within the walls of history. It's their relentless courage, tenacity, and defiance in the face of adversity that continue to inspire us. Be it in the arts, politics, sciences, literature, or basically everywhere, they leave an indelible imprint that sears through prejudice and discrimination.

Exploring Black Women's Emotional Strength and Resilience

Emotional strength and resilience are the secret sauce that has helped Black women endure the challenges of life and come out shining. This Swiss army knife of mental fortitude has proven particularly valuable for Black women, who have faced unique adversities across generations.

Picture this: the power of emotional strength in the form of a highly skilled Jedi knight. Armed with an invisible yet mighty force, emotional strength is the ultimate weapon that enables Black women to confront and overcome life's trials and tribulations. I mean, seriously, who wouldn't want to be a Jedi knight of emotional strength?

Now, let's talk about resilience, the dynamic sidekick of emotional strength. With resilience, Black women manage to bounce back from setbacks and emerge with newfound strength, courage, and wisdom. Sure, life may be playing a relentless game of Whac-a-Mole, but resilience allows Black women to pop back up, ready for whatever comes their way.

Little-known fact: Black women's perseverance is actually a combination of emotional strength and resilience that unequivocally screams, "I will not be broken!" Take, for instance, Madam C.J. Walker, the first Black female millionaire in the U.S., who built a beauty empire from the ground up in the early 20th century. Madam Walker faced countless obstacles, including financial struggles, racial barriers, and gender discrimination. But did she cower in fear or surrender? Absolutely not! She stood tall, fortified by an unyielding spirit and sheer determination, just like any superhero we know and love.

And let's not forget the tireless perseverance of civil rights activist Rosa Parks. When Parks refused to give up her bus seat in Montgomery, Alabama, in 1955, she didn't just spark a boycott and initiate the civil rights movement; she demonstrated insurmountable emotional strength.

But it doesn't stop there, folks. Black women have continued to demonstrate immense emotional strength and resilience well into the 21st century. Just look at former First Lady Michelle Obama, entrepreneur and philanthropist Oprah Winfrey, and world-class tennis star Serena Williams, who constantly defy expectations and shatter glass ceilings like it's nobody's business.

But this triumphant tale of emotional strength doesn't solely belong to the famous and successful. No, it resides in the hearts of countless Black women who face systemic racism, discrimination, and sexism every day. They are the unsung heroes who choose not to crumble beneath the weight of adversity but to stand tall and fight for a better future.

The victories of Black women from all walks of life serve as a testament to the immense power of emotional strength and resilience that lies within. They've managed to rise like phoenixes from the ashes of adversity, and their relentless march forward, filled with tenacity and grit, leaves a trail of inspiration in its wake.

A Tribute to Black Women Leaders and Role-models

Take a moment, close your eyes, strike the gong in the temple of your creative mind, and let us wade through an ocean of tenacity, resilience, and leadership dedicated to the magnificent Black women leaders and role models.

When we talk about successful Black women leaders, there's no shortage of names that echo through any chock-a-block room. From the awe-inspiring political dominance of Kamala Harris breaking the glass ceiling to the entrepreneurial genius of Oprah Winfrey, these extraordinary women have spoken louder than any barriers society might have erected. So, hail to these chiefs!

Alright, hold that thought! Imagine you're trekking up a mountain (don't start panting yet!). You're about halfway with no signs of the summit, and you're thinking of giving up when you see someone, a woman, in the far distance atop the peak. Now, that, my friends, is the impact of a role model, and Black women in society have become the indisputable beacon guiding the world through tough terrain. If Michelle Obama's grace didn't charm you, may I remind you of Mae C. Jemison? Stepping into her shiny NASA boots, she took a joyride to the stars, inspiring millions of little Black girls with cosmic dreams.

Let's gaze into this diverse galaxy of successful Black women across multiple fields, shall we? In sports, Serena Williams has left spectators utterly 'racketed' with her prowess. Meanwhile, in the literary arena, who can overlook the heart-wrenching narratives spun by Toni Morrison? And in the glossy corridors of fashion and beauty, we find the radiant Naomi Campbell and distinguished beauty mogul Pat McGrath, proving that Black is not just beautiful—it's stellar and far-reaching.

Let's not forget Aretha Franklin's R-E-S-P-E-C-T in music or Cicely Tyson redefining aging on screen. From the art of Faith Ringgold to the scientific breakthroughs of Marie M. Daly, these women have painted, sculpted, and scienced the heck out of their fields.

Now, before you accuse me of waxing poetic about Black women, understand this: when a child sees a role model who looks like them, it gives them the power to dream bigger. The canvas of society has been invigorated by the strokes of these Black women's genius and tenacity, challenging historical injustices and redefining norms.

In the hilarious words of Tiffany Haddish, "She ready!" and so are we, ready to see their trailblazing journeys raise the bar, ready to acknowledge their undying influence, and more than ready to celebrate every win in their columns!

From the 'take-no-nonsense' attitude of Shirley Chisholm to the soul-stirring voice of Beyoncé, you fine, strong, smart, and sassy Black women have made space for yourselves and are pulling up chairs for others. We acknowledge you. We root for you. We stand by you. Remember, folks, behind every successful woman, there's a squad of other successful women who have her back.

So, whether you are sitting in an office, lounging in your living room, or meeting a friend in the park, remember, you're twirling in the whirlwind unleashed by these trailblazing Black queens, and that, my friends, is something to celebrate. After all, as Viola Davis once said, the only thing that separates women of color from anyone else is opportunity. Here's to countless opportunities yet to come, and the Black women ready to seize them.

Unity in Diversity: The Way Forward

Bless your heart if you thought that the beauty of our diversity implies a lack of unity. Contrarily, in the grand mosaic of global citizens, it is the very nature of our differences that calls for unity. The society we inhabit is an awe-inspiring assortment of races, cultures, faiths, and lived experiences. Remember that time when you got a box of assorted chocolates and, united by your sweet craving, you savored each one despite the different flavors? There you go; you've practiced unity in diversity!

Examining the role of intersectionality in unity may elicit images of a bustling intersection in a big city, maybe because it sounds a bit like that. But hold your horses; it isn't about traffic management. Intersectionality covers various social categorizations like race, class, and gender, which overlap and intersect. Not clear yet? Imagine being a part of an ethnic minority, being a woman, and also being a part of the working class. Got it now? That's the intersectional highway we're talking about; it loads more taxing.

But here's the beauty of it. Intersectionality broadens our one-dimensional viewpoint and provides a clearer understanding of social inequality. It widens our perspective and helps us appreciate the full panorama of diverse experiences. So, in essence, it's like that XL pizza size upgrade for just 2 bucks more. It just offers more perspectives, more awareness, and more understanding without losing anything.

Now, let's dip our toes in the Kinross infinity pool of fostering collective progress through intersectionality. Kudos to those who have already used their free upgrade to the XL pizza and are reaping the benefits. For others, there is always time to acknowledge that collective progress is a somewhat mystical creature that can only be tamed by embracing diversity and intersectionality.

Let's either go down the memory lane or turn to the annals of history. A persistent reemergence of collective progress achieved through intersectionality would be clearer than your five-dollar fortune-teller's prophecy. Be it the Civil Rights Movement or the contemporary Black Lives Matter movement, it is the power of unity among diverse bodies, amplified by the multifaceted intersectional identities of the participants, that sets the ball rolling towards reformation and progress.

So, diversity isn't the marker dividing us; instead, it is akin to the various spices that blend together to prepare that perfect chicken curry. It is too mild, and it loses its character; too hot, and it loses its audience. Hence, it isn't diversity that threatens unity.

Let's take a grand lesson from fusion music, where a single tune embraces diverse rhythms and instruments yet delivers a harmonious symphony. So, to embrace our collective progress, let's be the fusion music in a world threatened by monotones. You see, unity in diversity is like the grand finale of an elaborate fireworks display. Each spark counts, every color matters, and what is the climax? A spectacle of intersectionality exploded into the night, leaving anyone standing beneath smitten with awe.

Let's take a moment to appreciate the role of Black women in driving this narrative. Through the sheer force of their resilience, they've set powerful precedents and been instrumental in their pursuit of unity in diversity.

CHAPTER 6: EMPOWERING BLACK WOMEN: HARNESSING TECHNOLOGICAL INNOVATION FOR SOCIAL CHANGE AND INCLUSIVE COMMUNITIES

Now, the role of Black women in technology—where do I begin? Firstly, we'd need a time-traveling DeLorean to track their countless achievements. Throughout history, they've made immense contributions to the tech world, innovating and advocating for inclusion and social change to ensure that the digital age is not just for the chosen few.

What's so significant about empowering Black women, you ask? Oh, just everything. When we empower Black women, we're essentially promoting socio-economic growth, inspiring younger generations, and setting the stage for an inclusive and revolutionary future.

Historical Significance of Black Women in Technology

Have you ever wondered why we don't see a Black Jane Bond in tech? Let me tell you, it's a genuine fight out there for Black women in the drilled-to-perfection male-dominated tech industry, from starters like 'Hey, doll. Can you fetch me a coffee?' to 'What do you know about coding?'—they've heard it all. It's not a Game of Thrones; it's more like a game of drones, and the drones are not playing nice.

But let's take a step back in history, get in our DeLorean, and travel to an era where technology was as cool as Justin Timberlake's '90s hair. That era had the brilliant minds of Black women such as Annie Easley and Katherine Johnson defying norms.

Easley wasn't just a human-computer—no, that's too mainstream. She was the human-lady-computer who worked on the Centaur rocket project—the launchpad for most of NASA's space probes. And dear Katherine Johnson made the famous astronomer John Glenn ask for her before he could twirl around Earth.

Moving forward, we land smack dab into the 21st century. Thankfully, the hair got better, and so did the opportunities for Black women in tech fields. We're still not doing the cha-cha down the street in celebration.

This is where women like Kimberly Bryant, the founder of Black Girls Code, and Sarah Kunst, the managing director of Cleo Capital, step in. Their achievements are milestones that echo in the hallways of every tech giant. Teaching young Black and brown girls to code and funding women in their entrepreneurial pursuits, these women are the modern knights in shining armor, albeit with keyboards instead of swords.

Bryant and Kunst aren't just the lone superheroines in this empowered lot of Black women in tech, oh no, siree. There's an army of modern wonder women out there, innovating, questioning, and conquering, one algorithm at a time, from Sheryl Sandberg, who's giving the reins to introverts to reach their full potential, to Dr. Arlyne Simon, an author, entrepreneur, and inventor patenting life-saving healthcare technology.

Maybe even, 'one small step for men, one giant leap for Black women." Too much? Well, this journey through the historical significance of Black women in the technology industry deserves a full-throttle exit.

The Intersection of Technology and Social Change

Like a young child discovering chocolate for the first time and forever associating it with unadulterated joy, the intersection of technology and social change is a treat that opens up worlds of possibilities, especially for Black women. Have you ever considered how technology is used for social justice and community building? How about a little thing called the internet and social media?

If there was an 'Oscars for Outstanding Performance in the Role of a Change Catalyst,' technology would shamelessly snag the trophy every single time! From contactless donations to protest coordination and giving voice to the voiceless (all while taking selfies, because why not?), technology's role in social change is as unmissable as Nollywood movies at a weekend family gathering.

Black women are not just sitting on the sidelines clapping. No, they're on the pitch, orchestrating the game! Look at how Black Lives Matter, a global movement started by three Black women, ingeniously leveraged technology to rally millions. Tweets and hashtags might seem trivial—until they bring down monuments and shake up systems. Patrice Cullors, Alicia Garza, and Opal Tometi bootstrapped a revolution with a #-tag, showing the world that Black women command the tech stage the same way Beyoncé owns... every stage.

Let's throw some more technology into the mix: e-commerce. This demon of digitization didn't just break the glass ceiling for Black women's entrepreneurship; it took the ceiling, fed it to the shredder, and used the shards to create a stylish glass mosaic artwork. From fashion to beauty to agriculture, Black women entrepreneurs are using the power of the internet to dismantle traditional barriers to market entry like an egg at breakfast time.

Remember the days when being an entrepreneur meant you had to actually have an office, employees (who never put the cap back on the coffee pot), and all those fun obstacles? No more. Thanks to online platforms, a Black woman entrepreneur can now set up a global e-business, smash sales records, and juggle family responsibilities all at the same time, all from the comfort of her own home.

But let's not forget one of our favorite pastimes: social media! It's hard to imagine how we survived before the era of hashtags, selfies, Instagram, and Twitter. (Probably by talking to each other or something old-fashioned like that.) But in this crazy, fast-paced digital world, social media has become a powerful tool for amplifying Black women's voices and causes.

Just ask Kimberly Bryant, founder of Black Girls Code. Through social media, she's raised the visibility of their work to teach coding skills to Black girls in marginalized communities, fighting for justice one line of code at a time. Then there's Opal Tometi, who, as a co-founder of the Black Lives Matter movement, knows a thing or two about using social media as a platform for revolutionary ideas.

In essence, if one glanced at the Rolodex of technological advancements championed for Black women, it would be filled with shining examples of software programs, apps, savvy businesses, and e-learning platforms that aim to encourage and empower.

And yet, let's not get complacent. The tech space still isn't exactly what you'd call a mecca of gender and racial equality. Technology is a tool, and like any tool, it's who wields it and how they wield it that counts. That's why championing Black women in tech is not just about saying, "Hey, look, Black women can do tech, too." It's about making sure they have the space, the resources, the support, and the agency to shape technology in ways that will fundamentally transform their lives and communities.

So, as we continue to peer into this revolutionary-looking glass, we must remain focused on championing inclusivity in the tech industry and bridging the digital divide for Black women. And as we raise our composed but fierce voices across digital platforms, let us constantly pay homage to the inspiring Black women and the vital roles they play, for as the saying goes, "When the game is changed, so do the players."

Promoting Inclusivity in the Tech Industry

Diversity and inclusivity in the tech workforce are not just trending hashtags. They're our sad, too-often-ignored necessities. Because, fun fact, tech isn't just the playground of awkward, serial killer-esque white guys living off ramen and mutual disdain. The more diverse the team, the wider the range of ideas, perspectives, and solutions.

Black women in tech are like hidden levels in a video game—few and far between, but when you find them, they're chock full of valuable goodies. This is all the more reason to treat them not like tokens but as talents that need recognition and nourishment. And that's where the second step comes in: mentorship and role models.

You know how it's easier to take a journey if there's someone showing the way, telling you about the potholes, dragons, and potential morale-destroying monsters ahead? That's exactly what mentorship does. Having Black women technopreneurs guide other Black women through the tricky maze of the industry is like holding a torch in the otherwise gloomy caves of tech giants' corridors.

Now you may wonder—where the heck are these mentors? Enter stage right, shining beacons of potentiality in the form of successful Black women in tech standouts like Kimberly Bryant, founder of Black Girls Code, and Angela Benton, founder and Chief Executive Officer of Streamlytics, to name just a couple. They are potential Yodas to the aspiring Luke Skywalkers (or should we say Luka Skywalkers?) in the tech galaxy.

Speaking of galaxies, it's high time we soared toward equal representation in STEM careers. It's not enough to just let Black women join the ranks; we need to make sure they're not treated like expendable red-shirts in the Star Trek space fleet. That means no more looking surprised when a Black woman is the tech lead or insisting they got the job 'because Black.' How about they got the job 'because brilliant'? Hmm?

Creating opportunities for Black women in tech isn't just about meeting diversity quotas or avoiding cultural controversies. It's a matter of recognizing talent that's been flying under the radar for way too long, much like our yet-undiscovered "Mars."

Bridging the Digital Divide for Black Women

Limited access to technology has dealt a heavy blow to Black women, akin to eating a veggie-loaded pizza—disappointing, right? Picture this: you have access to a world of opportunities at your fingertips, but because of your location, socio-economic status, and the color of your skin, you're locked out. Much like craving an exotic dessert after a sumptuous meal but realizing it's not on the menu. This is no dramatic screenplay; this is the stark day-to-day reality of many Black women. Technology, their literal "deus ex machina," which could uplift them economically and socially, often remains a distant dream due to systemic and infrastructural disparities.

Moving on, why should affordable internet access be as elusive as finding a parking spot in downtown Manhattan during rush hour? The lack of affordable internet and educational programs means that many Black women are left hanging on the cliffhanger of disrupted opportunities. It's like watching a potentially nail-biting thriller, but the climax gets canceled. Every cloud has a silver lining, right? Here come the rainmakers: initiatives like EveryoneOn and Digital Inclusion, among others, that are orchestrating symphonies of digital accessibility. They provide affordable internet services, devices, and training programs for marginalized communities. It's almost akin to having your cake and eating it too!

Well, talking about sharp left turns in our narrative, let's navigate toward gender-sensitive digital policies. Remember those instructions on an Ikea furniture package that leave you more puzzled than enlightened? That's how Black women often feel while dealing with obtuse digital policies. But what if these policies come with an easy-to-decipher manual targeting the specific needs of women? That's the essence of gender-sensitive digital policies and e-learning systems. Just imagine; it's like having your grandma explain a tricky recipe with step-by-step instructions versus wrestling alone with a vague YouTube tutorial. These policies consider the social, economic, and cultural conditions of Black women, enabling them to leap over digital hurdles with ease.

You see, this digital disparity saga may look like the miserable, rainy British weather, but every struggle is a breeding ground for resilience. Challenging? Absolutely! But you know what they say—tough times never last, but tough people do. And Black women, with their remarkable tenacity—finer than that seventy-year-old wine waiting to be uncorked—are proof positive of that adage.

Let's not forget the unconventional weapons in their digital arsenal: internet access in local libraries, free online courses and workshops, ICT training programs in communities, and a myriad of other resources. Black women, much like master chefs, are transforming these sparse ingredients into a culinary masterpiece of digital literacy.

Black women refuse to play the victim. They are the emerging heroines, fearlessly navigating the plot twists of the digital divide.

Inspiring Black Women in Tech

Okay, let's start with one name that left everyone spellbound: Kimberly Bryant. As the founder of Black Girls Code, she broke the mainstream mold and brought about a revolution in the Black community. Her non-profit organization is spinning the wheel of transformative change by providing young and pre-teen girls of color opportunities to learn in-demand skills in technology and computer programming. Talk about a superwoman multiplying into super girls - that's Kimberly Bryant and her amazing army for you! And dare you underestimate the power of the Black Girls Code. These tech divas aspire to train a million girls by 2050, and I don't think the 'Ctrl + Alt + Del' buttons are going to stop them.

Next up, we have Dr. Shirley Jackson, a theoretical physicist and the first Black woman to have earned a doctorate at the Massachusetts Institute of Technology (MIT). I mean, seriously, when I was a kid, I was struggling just to spell "Massachusetts." And here was Dr. Jackson, casually breaking barriers at MIT. But her impact goes even beyond her impressive credentials. She's well-known for the experiments that led to the creation of solar cells, fiber optic cables, and the technology behind caller IDs and call waiting. The sheer volume of phone calls today made possible by Dr. Jackson's work is astounding. Thank you, Dr. Jackson, for creating and innovating so that we may cyber-stalk our exes because, let's face it, traditional stalking is so passé.

Let's also take a moment to appreciate Dr. Mae Jemison, the first Black female astronaut. She hitched a ride with the Space Shuttle Endeavour and waved to us all from a galaxy far, far away. Note to self: You don't have to be a Star-Lord or a Jedi to visit space!

Now, I think it's valuable to remember that these leading ladies are not just tech pioneers; they are also torchbearers for underrepresented communities, and their efforts have inspired a generation of Black women to build a stronger presence in the tech industry. They've emphasized the point that every woman can code, just like every woman can cook. Their stories tell us that it's okay to be a woman in a man's world, it's okay to be Black in a white world, and, more importantly, it's fantastic to be a Black woman in the world of technology.

Building a career in tech isn't about being able to distinguish a microprocessor from a chocolate cookie at first glance. Instead, it's about having the grit to solve problems and the heart to break and reshape norms. Cliché as it may sound, yes, the glass ceiling has been shattered, and it's time to let the shards serve as a reminder for the upcoming generation of Black women technologists. The tech world is a deliciously coded pie, and every woman deserves a piece.

Remember, it's not just about coding and algorithms. It's about disrupting the norm, breaking stereotypes, and owning the throne. So, here's to all the Black women technologists out there—you are the Ada Lovelace, Grace Hoppers, and Katherine Johnsons of our generation.

CHAPTER 7: HEALTH EQUITY AND ACCESS: ADVOCATING FOR WELL-BEING AND DIGNITY

While strides in health advancements have been significant over the last century, you wouldn't believe (or maybe you would; we're not judging) that disparities in health outcomes as greasy as a diner burger persist. For Black women, the reality is even grimmer than dropping your last fry on the floor with no spare ones in sight.

On the topic of health disparities, it's not just an episode from a dystopian series. Nope, this is a real-life plot that's riding on the coattails of social and economic inequalities experienced by Black women. If you're thinking, "Well, it probably only concerns a handful of health issues," let me raise the curtain on this tragic play. Black women have to fight through excessive mortality rates, the boogeyman of shorter life expectancy, and horrifying rates of maternal mortality. If that wasn't enough to rattle your nerves, let's throw chronic conditions like anemia, CVD, and obesity into the mix.

The tale of Black women's health in the U.S., let me tell you, is not woven with silken threads of equality and justice; it's more like a rickety bridge made from frayed ropes of racial disparity and gender discrimination, swaying precariously above the river of historical racial abuse. From being forcefully coerced into reproduction during the slavery era to enduring unethical biomedical experiments under the name of 'gynecology research,' Black women's health journey through time is a patchwork quilt of terrifying stories, each more harrowing than the last.

The aim is not to churn your stomach but to shed light on the persistent health inequities among Black women and to highlight the structural contributors that pave the runway for these disparities.

The Layered Onion of Health Disparities Faced by Black Women

Let's rip off the facade and probe what's happening under the guise of racial and social determinant factors. The big question is, "Why are Black women three times more likely to die during childbirth?" Isn't that like signing up for a game of Russian roulette each time they decide to bask in the blessing of motherhood?

Well, here's a slice of our notorious social structure's cold reality: a deep-rooted racial bias. Black women are presumed less likely to adhere to prescriptions—with no evidence other than skin color. Sometimes, I, too, hope someone can prescribe medication for ignorance, but pharmacies don't stock that!

Now, I wish I could say you adorn your rose-tinted glasses. However, the socio-economic disadvantages and their influence on health are somewhat like a chronic itch; you ignore it, and it welcomes a full-blown infection. What fancy term do we give to the chronic suffering of Black women from the wages of neglect? Perhaps "economic itis?" This heavyweight makes life expectancies shorter and invites uninvited guests of anemia, cardiovascular diseases, and obesity.

Our journey into this 'layered onion' unveils one heart-wrenching layer after the other. Maternal mortality statistics among Black women are no less harrowing than a tragic opera, filled with pain and sorrow, in which the lady doesn't just lose her love; she loses her life. We are looking at higher rates of maternal mortality compared to their non-Black counterparts, my friends, three to fourfold! At this rate, it seems delivering babies has turned into some ogre-ish birthing roulette.

Unfortunately, that's not all. This layered labyrinth dives deeper, unmasking the unnerving racial disparities in chronic conditions. Let me lay some irony on you: Black women stand proud as the superhumans managing households despite unimaginable obstacles; unfortunately, their bodies bear the price. Be it heart disease, cancer, or diabetes, it's like they've been handpicked for this catastrophic health lottery, except nobody wants to win!

In contrast, Cinderella's fairy godmother only worked magic with a pumpkin and a pair of rodents. In our tale, Black women, juggling socio-economic pressures with a dysfunctional healthcare system's bias, continue to battle chronic conditions with evolving strain. It's not just a medical issue; it's a societal disease that impacts kings and paupers alike.

In a nutshell, here we are in the 21st century, waving our hands toward outer space and curing cancers, yet grappling with fundamental health disparities is like trying to catch smoke with a bare hand.

Exploring the Structural Factors that Compound Health Disparities

The healthcare system is a place where everyone, regardless of race or gender, is supposed to receive equal treatment, at least in theory. But when it comes to Black women, reality seems to have gotten lost in the memo. There's an undeniable, persistent bias, both conscious and unconscious, towards Black women within healthcare institutions. And we're not just talking about doctors and nurses cracking jokes at the expense of Black women—although, not cool, by the way. No, we're talking about life-and-death disparities that directly affect Black women's health outcomes.

Have you ever heard of the notorious Tuskegee Syphilis Study? Or the forced sterilization of Black women in the 20th century? Buckle up, because these dark and twisted tales are just a glimpse into the murky depths of biomedical research involving Black women. It's like an episode of Black Mirror, but, you know, real life.

For years, Black women were subjected to horrific, non-consensual, and non-therapeutic medical experiments that made Dr. Frankenstein look like a saint. The wholesale exploitation of Black women's bodies for the advancement of medical knowledge is a stark reminder of just how devalued and disposable society once considered them—and, sadly, some aspects haven't changed much.

Picture this: A Black woman enters a clinic, expressing concerns about her health. Healthcare provider A doesn't take her symptoms seriously, dismissing her as exaggerating. Healthcare provider B makes assumptions about her lifestyle choices, judgment dripping from every meticulously crafted question. Healthcare provider C seems spaced out—hey, maybe they've been binge-watching Grey's Anatomy too much. Our Black woman leaves feeling unheard, unseen, and untreated. Rinse and repeat.

And then there's childbirth. You thought bringing new life into the world was all about pastel-colored baby showers and impossibly tiny onesies? Think again. For many Black women, it's a harrowing and dangerous experience. Severe maternal morbidity rates are alarmingly higher for Black women, with some health professionals apparently still subscribing to the long-debunked myth that they experience less pain—we're not kidding; it's the end of 2023, and this is still a thing.

So, as we peel back the layers of this messy onion, it becomes clear that health equity for Black women cannot be achieved without addressing these deep-rooted biases, disparities, and discrimination within the healthcare system. And, while it's tempting to throw in the towel and drown our sorrows in a pint of ice cream, this fight is far from over. The resilience and strength of Black women shine through even the bleakest moments, and change is possible—one sarcastic quip, sarcastic chuckle, and empathetic action at a time.

As they say, laughter is the best medicine, but it alone won't fix decades of systemic failures. We need understanding, empathy, and an unwavering commitment to dismantling the systems perpetuating harm and inequality.

Peeling Back the History: Examining the Roots of the Current Crisis

If the sea of health disparity is an onion, then by all means, let's bravely tear off a few layers and toss a bit of history over our shoulders while we mince it to find the hidden truth.

Maybe you thought gynecology was like a cakewalk with stirrups and speculums. It's more of a haunted house ride. Cloaked in the shadowy shrouds of the 1850s, the esteemed field of gynecology was born (pun intended). This grand chapter of "medical advancements" was written in the blood and tears of Black women used as guinea pigs without the common decency of asking for consent. Honestly, even zombies wouldn't sink so low.

No, this isn't a sci-fi horror film. It's as real as the overpriced popcorn you are probably chewing. Black women were subjected to excruciating experiments so we could learn about life passing through the birth canal. No wonder some spirits are still wandering around medical school classrooms.

Alright, enough of the gory stuff. Let's switch gears to an even darker period (because we haven't upset you enough). Have you heard of a little thing called slavery? Oh, you have? Excellent. Thank you, American education system. What they conveniently left out, of course, is the detailed explanation of how it essentially kicked down the door and strolled into the health of Black women.

Like a reincarnated Voldemort, the specter of slavery has cast long, dark shadows over the health of Black women. Health disparity among Black women found its roots in slavery, when Black women were seen as nothing more than economic assets for white slaveholders. For Simba, life was the "circle of life"; for Black women, it was circular exploitation—being - forced to breed with their reproductive rights trampled all over and minimal healthcare to boot.

And when you think your tear ducts have gotten a break, here comes another paragraph. Fight the urge to wave a white flag because we're speaking about the never-ending battle for reproductive justice. Here's a bit of irony for you: while white women were fighting for the liberty to prevent pregnancies, Black women were struggling to have their pregnancies valued. Imagine having to put a price tag on life.

The fight for reproductive justice has been long and hard and continues. Continued marginalization and disregard for the health and bodies of Black women have kicked up enough dust to kickstart a whole movement. But we aren't talking about a weekend of picketing and nicely worded signs; we're talking about a long-term, gloves-off, no-holds-barred, '80s montage-worthy struggle. It's Rocky Balboa, with a hint of Rosa Parks and a pinch of Maya Angelou. In a world that continues to hit them down, Black women continue to resist, persist, and rise superheroes without capes.

We've peeled back the historical layers to unveil the bitterness of the health disparities experienced by Black women. We hope you've taken notes, learned a few things, and shed some tears for these women's plight and strength.

The Ongoing Public Health Emergency: A Closer Look at the Maternal Mortality Crisis

The joy of motherhood is the magical, mystical experience of bringing new life into the world. For most women, it's a time of wonder, excitement, and anticipation. But for Black women in the United States, it can be a death sentence.

You read that right. Black women are three to four times more likely to die during pregnancy or childbirth than white women. So, while white women are checking out swanky strollers and organic baby food, Black women are rolling the dice with their very lives. It sounds pretty serious, doesn't it? Spoiler alert: it is.

But what is the source of these dismal statistics, you ask? The story of non-Hispanic Black women caught in the Maternal Mortality Crisis and the tug of war between physical and mental health disparities, all tied up in a neat little package with an "inextricable link" bow on top.

First on our tour of despair: Non-Hispanic Black Women and the Maternal Mortality Crisis. All other things being equal, a simple switcheroo of skin tones shouldn't make that much of a difference, right? Wrong! The stark contrast in maternal mortality rates among racial groups is a stark sign of deep-rooted health inequities that desperately need to be addressed. So, here we find ourselves, neck-deep in a crisis driven by systemic disparities and missed opportunities in healthcare.

Chronic conditions like cardiovascular disease, obesity, and mental health issues run rampant among Black women, exacerbated by social, economic, and environmental factors. And to cap it all off, these physical and mental health disparities aren't just holding hands and taking a leisurely stroll through the park. Oh, no. They're piggybacking on one another, becoming more than just the sum of their parts.

Picture it: interconnected threads, forming a web of woes and misery, all starting with good old systemic racism and inequality. Our girl in the hot seat finds herself straddling this precarious tightrope, attempting to balance the weight of societal expectations and ever-present health threats, all while bearing the burden of her own self-advocacy in healthcare settings.

But wait, "What about personal responsibility?" "A healthy lifestyle and positive attitude can fix anything, right?" While I'm sure our yoga mats and green smoothies are doing wonders for our Instagram-worthy glows, it just isn't enough to dismantle the deeply ingrained system of inequity at the root of these disparities.

As the curtain closes on our tale of sorrow, we're left with a sobering realization: this is a fight we're all in together. At the heart of the matter, we need to dissect and address the structural factors that contribute to these disparities while giving a standing ovation to the incredible Black women who've faced these challenges head-on and still stand tall, advocating for change.

So, what can we do? Raise awareness. Speak up. Support policies that promote health equity and access for all. After all, it shouldn't take a miracle for Black women to bring new lives into the world safely.

Advocating for Health Equity: A Movement Spearheaded by Black Women

Social and economic equity is like saying, "Hey, let's give everyone the same shot at a good life," but in corporate speak, it fits in PowerPoint presentations. Because who wouldn't love that? In a world where being a Black woman doesn't feel like you've been given the 'try hard mode' in the game of life, It's more like 'healthcare inequity'—a classic sequel to 'Racism: The Prequel,' right?

Sadly, this isn't a game. It's real life. And in real life, Black women have been pulling up their boots and leading the frontline battle for health equity like the absolute bosses they are. They've been shattering the glass ceiling, refusing to be confined by the lower shelf in the healthcare pantry. For example, you've got Black women doctors dedicating their careers to research focused on racial health disparities. Isn't that like double jeopardy? Fighting the system from inside the system is pretty unique, if you ask me.

But Black women aren't just making strides in healthcare; they're practically running a marathon—and not one of those fancy ones where you get a cool medal at the end. Shoutouts to the Black nurses, healthcare providers, and advocates who form an unstoppable task force against those pesky health disparities.

And let's not forget racial bias and gender discrimination, the 'Bonnie and Clyde' of social issues. They're like that annoying couple at a party who overstay their welcome, making everyone uncomfortable with their toxic behavior. But what is the impact on Black women in health institutions? It's like having to put up with Bonnie and Clyde's passive-aggressive commentary while trying to perform an intricate ballet. You know, the kind where a misstep could cost lives.

Yet, somehow, Black women handle it, day in and day out. They endure, advocate, educate, and heal while fighting a system grudging to give them even an inch. It's like they've been handed a sword to fight in a gun battle, but still, they refuse to back down. So, yes, we're talking about racial bias, gender discrimination, and social inequity—not because they're catchy phrases, but because we see these obstacles every day. But remember, behind these issues stands a legion of Black women, ready to take them down and rewrite history.

So, here's to the Black women making a difference in healthcare and pushing for health equity—doing the Macarena around the elephant in the room isn't going to make it disappear. Kudos to the real-life superheroes—you gals are the 'Marvel' we need. To quote Beyoncé, "Who runs the world?" Girls!" More specifically, Black women are running the healthcare world and doing a good job at it too!

In a world that seems to have a peculiar obsession with onions, these champions keep peeling back layers and layers of health disparities. But this fight is still ongoing, and like a never-ending marathon, we've still got laps to go.

Support organizations and initiatives working towards health equity. Actions speak louder than words, and money talks even louder. There is no need to break your piggy bank; even a small contribution can go a long way.

As we cruise to the end of our journey, let's raise a metaphorical glass to Black women who have made strides in healthcare and forge ahead in advocating for health equity. Remember, with power comes responsibility—or was it the other way around? Either way, it's time to give the superheroes we call "Black women" the backup they deserve.

CHAPTER 8: FINANCIAL INDEPENDENCE AND ECONOMIC EMPOWERMENT: PATHWAYS TO PROSPERITY FOR BLACK WOMEN

You see, the importance of economic empowerment for Black women stretches beyond Thanos' ability to snap his fingers. When offered equitable opportunities, Black women can elevate themselves, their families, and communities towards self-sufficiency, which would make any action hero green with envy.

Our dear Black women face several barriers in their quest for financial independence. Systemic racism and sexism have built seemingly insurmountable walls, barring access to resources, opportunities, and fair treatment. Like a cosmic super-villain, these dark forces manifest in wealth inequality, limited access to capital for potential business owners, and a restricted ability to climb the economic ladder.

Historical Context

The ever-so-fine "Racial and Gender Wealth Gap" is a classic example of a problem older than the ancient Egyptian pyramids. Black women have had it rough! They not only face racial barriers, but let's throw in some gender discrimination for good measure. This fabulous combo results in the shocking statistic that Black households have just 15 percent of the wealth of white households.

"Is it a bird?" Is it a plane? "No, it's systemic racism and sexism in the US." Over here, we have white supremacy and sexism working in tandem to ensure that Black women's labor is devalued and suppressed for centuries. Remember when we said that the racial wealth gap was larger than the income gap? Well, guess what? Both of these gaps are widened by systemic racism and sexism!

Now, let's talk about numbers. Single Black female heads of households with a college degree have 38 percent less wealth than their white counterparts with no degree. Married Black women who are head of the household don't get it any easier—they have 79 percent less wealth than white women with no degree and a staggering 83 percent less wealth than white women with a degree.

If these stats were movie sequels, they would probably be called

"The Never-Ending Nightmare: How We Let Black Women Down" and its sequel, "The Perpetual Betrayal of Black Women."

Financial Strategies for Black Women

We all know, "There's no place like home." But what if that home could also make you money? Aha! Yes, we're talking about wealth-building through—wait for it—homeownership. But wait, it's not as simple as Dorothy clicking her red heels. It requires the elimination of second mortgages, which are often more treacherous than a tornado. We must recognize the significance of creating and preserving affordable housing. After all, buying a home shouldn't resemble an episode of "Mission Impossible," right? So, it's a rallying cry: cheaper housing for all, and to all, a good night!

Enough of houses, though; let's leap into our shiny business suits and talk about the alluring 'Access to Capital.' What's that? Well, it's like going to the supermarket and realizing that you have an unlimited food budget. Whoa! Can you imagine the endless aisle of cheese you could buy? Sadly, this doesn't exactly exist in the real world. For many Black women business owners, access to capital is a well-guarded treasure chest they've been trying to unlock for ages. And to those firms owned by Black women, remember that the power lies within you (and in a suite of financial instruments)! Grants for startups, loans, angel investments, venture capital, blended financing, factoring—you name it, they've got it. It's like a buffet of investment options, so don't be afraid to fill your plate.

Regarding investment options, next on our agenda is 'Navigating Financial Instruments for Business Growth." You might think I'm about to talk about flutes and drums, but how wrong you are. We're treading on the path of everything from bonds, stocks, derivatives, deposits, and loans like a financial Indiana Jones. Remember, startups are about 'finding' these instruments and expertly playing them for optimal growth. It's time to learn the symphony of success.

But you thought we were done? Oh, no. This game of Monopoly isn't wrapped up that easily. The final cherry on this sundae is being able to provide firms owned by Black women access to these financial instruments at all stages of the business cycle. I mean, you can't ride a bike without wheels, right?

Reading that might make it seem like you just ran a financial marathon, but remember, it doesn't end here. Just like Rihanna says, "Work, work, work," let's also say, "Invest, invest, invest." And while adding more zeros to those bank statements, don't forget to enjoy every bit of the journey. When those investments pay off, that sense of accomplishment is comparatively more satisfying than finishing a whole pizza yourself. Almost, anyway.

Addressing Student Loan and Medical Debt

Student loans are the gift that keeps on taking. And Black college-educated women are bearing an especially heavy burden when it comes to student loan debt. That's one way to close the beloved racial and gender wealth gap, right? You see, such debt actually perpetuates the gap by hindering wealth accumulation.

So, the brilliant idea of canceling student loan debt is gaining some traction—for good reason. We're giving Black women a fair shot at economic stability and mobility by lifting this massive, growing burden. And while we're at it, let's not forget that fun little thing called medical debt that's also doing its part to gnaw away at their wealth. You know, to make things equal and all.

Addressing the wealth gap starts with admitting we have a problem, and let's face it, medical debt is quite the problem for Black women. Due to disproportionately poor health later in life, they face mounting medical bills that do an excellent job of evaporating any wealth they've managed to accumulate. And don't even get me started on the difficulty of intergenerational wealth transfer.

But, instead of complaining about it, let's talk about solutions. How about canceling medical debt, too? Let's cut them some slack so they can build wealth without that nagging feeling that their next medical bill could gravely erase it all.

Now, don't get too excited just yet. While canceling student loans and medical debt might sound like the answer to all our prayers, it's not enough. We need policy changes to make a difference, and we need them now. We've got to shake up the systems that have perpetuated these inequalities and say, "Enough is enough! We're done playing this game."

To do that, let's start with implementing solutions that specifically target the structural racism and sexism that put Black women at a disadvantage when it comes to debt accumulation. Policies should actively protect them from predatory lending practices and exorbitant interest rates that only serve to plunge them deeper into the red.

And how about standing up for some concrete measures to make higher education more accessible and affordable? Come on, it's high time we traded those insanely high tuitions for some good old-fashioned, fairer investments in education that don't force Black women to literally mortgage their futures.

As for medical debt, it's time for a healthcare system overhaul that treats everyone fairly, regardless of their race or gender. A system that ensures access to quality, affordable healthcare for everyone, especially those who may not have other means to pay for necessary treatments. It sounds revolutionary, but let's keep dreaming big here.

In the meantime, what can we do to chip away at the barriers faced by Black women in achieving financial independence and economic empowerment? For starters, we can support the philanthropic efforts and investments of organizations like Goldman Sachs. With initiatives like their One-Million Black Women project, they're investing significant capital to address these very issues.

So, imagine a world where student loans and medical debt are no longer barriers to financial freedom for Black women. It's a possibility if we all step up and work together. By implementing policy changes and supporting initiatives designed to bridge the wealth gap, we can create a more equitable society where everyone has a fair shot at prosperity. And isn't that a world worth fighting for?

Impact of Philanthropy and Investments

We thought philanthropy only belonged to the billionaires' club, but Goldman Sachs' One-Million Black Women initiative flipped the script. Using its deep pockets ($10 million to be swiped from), this initiative aims to lift Black women out of the economic Black hole and onto the train of progress and prosperity.

But wait, is that just another philanthropic daydream? Nope! Goldman Sachs did their homework by going on a four-month listening tour—an actual "have an ear" kind of tour. And who were they listening to? The beautiful, strong, and resilient Black women across the country. These community advocates, small business owners, corporate leaders, union workers, and academicians all had a lot to say. So, they partnered with the Urban Institute to funnel these voices into actionable steps toward closing the wealth gap. Talk about empowering the very community you are aiming to uplift!

One can never have too many friends or too many solutions to economic empowerment. The idea here is to dismantle structural racism and develop solutions that actually make sense and benefit those most affected. And how do we do that? Investing in community organizations that know the neighborhood inside out like no one else does.

Okay, enough of the astonishment. What if we told you other organizations were hopping onto the empowerment wagon? Surprising as it might be, it looks like holding hands and working together is becoming a thing. The more, the merrier, right? So, we witness the growth of philanthropic efforts by various entities that pour heart (and money) into creating a more equitable society. The idea is to support education, businesses, and leadership opportunities for Black women. Cheers to a rising collective consciousness!

One might think that a philanthropic boom will do the trick. Well, not quite. While our charming Black women deserve the pink carpet to succeed, who needs red or blue? This doesn't mean sitting back and relaxing while someone else paves the way. The Urban Institute and Goldman Sachs know the power lies within these women, and that's the very reason they went on that listening tour we recently gossiped about. So yes, investments and philanthropy are crucial, but the real magic happens when Black women themselves take charge and build their future.

So, here we are, with the impactful role of philanthropy and investments in empowering Black women. Multiple initiatives and community-based solutions are budding, and they're creating a more equitable, inclusive, and just society. But progress truly shines when Black women take the reins of changing themselves and being that force of nature we know they've been all along.

Creating Systemic Change

Firstly, those pesky policy recommendations to dismantle structural racism. It's almost laughable how our society has been built on a foundation of inequality. It's like constructing a tower on a jello mold—bound to crumble sooner or later. So, number one on our to-do list? Dismantle it all, brick by racist brick. Let's not just put a band-aid on a bullet wound. It's time for full-blown surgery. It's about creating inclusive policies that serve all communities, not just the privileged few. Hey, we're all for equal opportunities, right?

Plus, we've got some action points! Let's start by addressing income disparities by implementing a universal basic income. And how about an unconditional apology attached to reparations for slavery? Sounds radical, right? But radical problems require radical solutions.

Imagine a world where everyone starts on an even playing field, where your skin color doesn't determine your bank balance. It sounds crazy, doesn't it? But guess what? It's possible! Oprah wasn't built in a day, you know.

A key lever to this transformation? Education. And no, not the stuffy, outdated textbook education that taught you that the mitochondria are the cell's powerhouse. Who cares? We're talking about an education that encourages critical thinking and empathy and dismantles prejudice from the root. It's about creating human beings, not just products of an outdated, assembly-line schooling system.

And finally, let's talk about activism. Many dismiss it as a bunch of hippies yelling at buildings, but it's much more than that. It's a catalyst for change. The trembling voice confronts the oppressor and the shaking hands that hold the placard high. Activism is when you decide that the "status quo" just isn't good enough anymore.

Without activism, those policy recommendations wouldn't see the light of day, and our dream of an equitable society would be just that—a dream. From the Suffragettes to Black Lives Matter, these movements have fueled social change, proving that a whisper can indeed become a roar if delivered with unyielding determination.

So, yes, we have a long way to go. But remember, Rome wasn't built in a day. And while we're on the subject, did you know that Ancient Rome was the brainchild of Romulus, whom a wolf raised? I'm just saying that if a wolf-raised dude could create Rome, we could surely create a more equitable society, right? What's it going to take? It's just a combination of radical policy changes, a revamp of education, and tons of loud and courageous activism!

CHAPTER 9: LEGACY AND INSPIRATION: HONORING CONTRIBUTIONS AND SHAPING FUTURES OF BLACK WOMEN IN HISTORY AND BEYOND

What do we mean by legacy and inspiration, you ask? Well, legacy is what these phenomenal women leave behind—the torch they pass on, the impact they've etched into history's walls. Inspiration? It's that warm, fuzzy feeling that tugs at our hearts, the stirring in our bellies, and the inner voice that whispers, "Hey, maybe I can do something amazing too!"

"But what does it have to do with Black women?" you might ask. Well, let me tell you, human history is teeming with the courage, resilience, and fortitude of Black women who've pushed boundaries and shattered glass ceilings, leaving a lasting impact on our world. Do you feel the ground quaking beneath you yet? That's the power of these women!

The Struggle, The Win: Phenomenal Historical Black Women

Harriet Tubman bulldozed through the infamous days of slavery, not only securing her freedom but also creating a scenic route and an underground railroad for others. What is the tuition fee for this life-or-death tour? Nope, not a dime! Talk about ultimate community service (and with no tips accepted, either!). Moving on to our dear Rosa Parks, the ultimate queen of bus travel. Nope, she didn't invent a teleportation device, but she stood (or rather sat) against racial discrimination, sparking a revolution that makes your daily bus commute less, let's say, segregated.

Now, sprinting to the final lap of our history marathon, we marvel at the wonder woman, Shirley Chisholm. She went all-in at the political poker table, smashing through racial and gender barriers, and becoming the first African American woman elected to the U.S. Congress. And let's not forget her audacious campaign for the presidency. Did she lose? The important part is that she ditched the kitchen, invaded the political arena, and sprinkled some much-needed diversity (and sass!).

Your heart is pounding with awe, admiration, and probably a bit of envy – am I right? But these phenomenal ladies weren't just putting up a show to sell tickets for a movie. They were shifting the tectonic plates of society, causing shocking waves of change.

Tubman's bravery and altruism not only freed hundreds of slaves but also swiped left on the concept of racial inferiority. Parks? She spurred a boycott that fast-forwarded America into the Civil Rights era. And let's not forget our trailblazer, Chisholm, who cleverly shoved the door wide open for Black women in politics. So, next time you see a Black woman in leadership, give a little nod to our old friend, Shirley.

Regarding societal impact, remember the domino effect, where a small change triggers a cascade of transformations? That's exactly what these "gravity-defying" ladies achieved. The strong, happily vibrant, sassy, and occasionally loud (because why shouldn't they be?) Black woman you encounter today? Oh, you have our historical miracle workers to thank for that!

So, what more do these relentless, life-altering, ceiling-shattering, and occasionally bus-preferring leading ladies have to teach us? Well, do yourself a favor.

Say it Loud: The Contemporary Strong Black Women.

Each one is an exquisite mosaic of courage, strength, resilience, and beauty—we landed on the essence of today's Black woman. A successful CEO, an influential activist, a proud athlete, or an illustrious scientist—you name it, Black women are brilliantly shining in all spheres of life. Believe it or not, they are shaking and shaping the world, one stride at a time, because 'Hey! Why should Beyoncé have all the fun?

But wait, it's not all rainbows and cupcakes. These ladies encounter challenges that could make even the bravest souls think twice. But "twice" isn't part of their vocabulary. Today's Black woman faces the world head-on, weaponizing stereotypes as motivation, winning battles against inequality, and unshackling societal expectations. It's like watching Wonder Woman, only ten times better because this isn't Cinemax; it's real life!

So, what's their superpower? Maybe it's their strength in the roots of their diligent work ethic. Or it's the audacity they manifest when they voice their thoughts without fear of judgment. But let's not forget the unspoken magic these women possess—metamorphosing the challenges and adversities they face into steppingstones, paving their way toward relentless progress. If "adversity breeds genius," these women are the Albert Einstein of overcoming challenges.

And yes! It's high time we recognized these unsung heroines for their laudable contributions to society. Look around and hear their names echoing in the hallways of achievement: Serena Williams breaking records on tennis courts, Kamala Harris adding a touch of color to the White House, and Chimamanda Ngozi Adichie writing African characters into mainstream literature. It's like they have their own superhero league, and there's no kryptonite strong enough to defeat them.

From business, politics, and sports to art and culture, in every domain, Black women are reshaping narratives and smashing glass ceilings into oblivion, all while juggling multiple roles. And when you think you have seen it all, they raise the bar a bit higher. It's as if they're part of this secret "Raise the Bar" club. We're just waiting for the membership form to leak.

But let's be real; these women aren't striving for glory or fame. They're on a mission to build a legacy and inspire future Black women, proving to them and the rest of the world that their dreams are valid, attainable, and very much worth it.

As we ride this wave of exuberance, let's not overlook a vital truth: these contemporary, phenomenal Black women are crafting a new way forward. We're lucky to witness their journey and, hopefully, absorb a little of their magic along the way.

Black Girl Magic: Empowering Legacies in the Spotlight

What in the world is "Black Girl Magic"? Oh, it's just a small movement that redefines the resilience and excellence of Black women. It's like finding out that your DNA has strands of wonder-woman-ness woven into it. Who knew?

The term itself is a shout-out to all the Black women who've turned life's lemons into lemonade so good that even Beyoncé would want a sip. It's about celebrating the extraordinary within the ordinary—the moms, the CEOs, the artists, and every Black queen conquering battles both in the spotlight and the shadows.

And speaking of spotlights, let's not forget the legends who've left legacies so powerful that they've become the North Stars for young Black girls navigating their own journeys. Take Maya Angelou, for example. The woman penned words that could hug you, heal you, and give you a stern talking to—all at the same time. Then there's Shirley Chisholm, who waltzed into the U.S. Congress and became its first Black woman member, adding a whole new level of finesse to the world of politics.

But legacies aren't just about the past; they whisper sweet nothings into the future's ear, inspiring the next lineup of Black leading ladies. The impact of such legacies is akin to the domino effect, but instead of falling down, each domino rises taller than the last.

Imagine that young girl in her bedroom, wide-eyed, as she watches Kamala Harris become the first female, first Black, and first South Asian vice president of the U.S. That's a future painted with ambition and shades of "Yes, I can." It's women like her, and of course, our forever FLOTUS Michelle Obama, who embodies the elegance and intelligence that redefine what power looks like—not just a pretty face, but a formidable force equipped with an education, compassion, and the sassiness to tell it like it is.

And what about influence, huh? Well, imagine influence as that cool aunt who crashes the family BBQ, and everyone can't help but mimic her style, walk, and talk. That's what these empowering Black women's legacies are for future generations. They set trends without even trying, breaking cultural ceilings with a sledgehammer of sophistication.

Now, take a second and visualize the worlds of music, film, literature, and science—every nook and cranny of life, really—sprinkled with the essence of Black female empowerment. It's like adding hot sauce to your favorite dish. It brings the heat and the flavor and leaves you wondering how you ever lived without it.

But let's not hold hands and sing 'Kumbaya' just yet because there are still oceans to cross. The good news? Each legacy is a lifesaver, keeping Black women afloat in those oceans. And let no one tell you that Black women are only defined by their struggles—no, they're also the fantasy, the dream, and the hard-earned reality worth celebrating.

So, what does this all mean for you? If you're a young Black woman, remember—you're standing on the shoulders of giants, so reach for the stars with the confidence of one who's destined to shine. And if you're not, that's cool too; make sure you're cheering loud enough from the sidelines and passing the mic when it's time.

Black Girl Magic isn't a one-hit wonder. It's a timeless album on repeat, providing the soundtrack to a movement that sees Black women as they are: sorceresses in their own tales, turning what was once invisible into a legacy of visibility and pride that will resonate far into the future. And that kind of magic doesn't just dazzle—it lights the way.

Moving Forward: The Future of Black Women

Firstly, trends and predictions Ladies and gentlemen, bend over and tie your shoelaces because the next wave of Black female trailblazers is bursting onto the scene, and they're running like they've stolen Usain Bolt's lightning! From boardrooms to courtrooms, Kente to couture, and politics to indoor picnics—they're here, they're fierce, and boy, oh boy, they're not waiting for an invite!

Bringing along a duffle bag of determination, wit, and the secret sauce to success, they're gearing up to explode stereotypes like glitter bombs. And let me tell you, I can't wait to see that rain of brilliance!

However, here come the obstacles and opportunities. What's that? Obstacles? Oh, you mean those annoying little speed bumps that look terrifying but actually catapult you to greater heights? Yes, we see them. But let's spill the tea: they're like the villains in a superhero movie—scary until the hero pulls out her invincible superpowers. And do you know the kryptonite to these obstacles? It's an opportunity!

Armed with education, enlightenment, and empowerment (the three E's of evolution; I just made that up, patent pending), Black women are not just dodging obstacles but doing some gravity-defying, Matrix-style leap over them. They're also turning blocks into springboards to soar into an ocean of opportunities.

Now, inhale deeply because we're plunging into Inspiration Central, folks. Let's talk about inspiring the next generation. The task is as monumental as trying to calculate the number of pearl-shaped stars in the night sky. But Black women? They have that job all wrapped up!

Now, you better sit down for this, or you might stumble over in awe. From moms to moguls, mentors to teachers, and icons to online influencers, whether they're baking cupcakes or breaking glass ceilings, Black women are molding the mindset of the new generation with their can-do attitude, their courageous spirits, and their steadfast commitment to change.

Much like snapping a photo of Bigfoot, capturing the magnificence of the future of Black women is nothing short of magical. Their legacies are like constellations: bright, beautiful, and guiding the way like never before.

Monumental Shift: The Role of Society

Have you ever met society? Yes, you heard right. Meet her, the 'she' who wields an immense power to make or break, to stand with you in solidarity, or to isolate you in a corner. An uninvited guest at your dinner table, a relentless critic in your artistic pursuits, a boisterous cheerleader when you win, and an 'I told you so' murmur when you fall. But what happens when society, the one usually known for parading around in 'status quo' couture, decides to wear 'change' as her style statement? Let's delve right in, shall we?

So, here's society, strutting down the lane, notorious for being a stereotypical drama queen. Picture that: she loves her cookie-cutter shapes and is fond of painting everyone with the same brush. Well, 'presumption' is her favorite pastime, and 'stereotype' is her best friend.

How's that for an image? A privilege check for society, for a change! That's right; the astronomical shift is to view Black women not as a monolithic group but as individuals with unique experiences, capabilities, and aspirations. Much like breaking down the Berlin Wall, this shift is about dismantling concrete beliefs one brick at a time.

Erasing stereotypes is as easy as dieting; everyone knows what to do, but few actually do it. Society needs to get off that comfy stereotype couch and hit the treadmill, breaking a serious sweat in the 'equality' gym!

Quick question. Who doesn't love a good tug-of-war? Yes, the quintessential pull between man and woman, Black and white, rich and poor, yin and yang, the 'Us vs. Them.' You've probably seen it, been there, done that, and bought the T-shirt. But wait, isn't it overrated? What if we switched from tug-war to line dancing, from 'vs.' to 'and,' from 'either-or' to 'yes' Swapping confrontation for collaboration—that's promoting equality!

Next, we unveil society's newest look: female empowerment. Is there a hashtag for that aside from #Unbelievable and #AboutTime? You see, empowerment is that sparkling, irresistible perfume that a Black woman wears, turning heads as she walks, eliciting respect and, dare we say it, awe. The shine in her eyes, the stride in her step, and the fierce spirit that refuses to be tamed.

Imagine society cheering on, encouraging Black women to step into their power, climb the corporate ladder, lead countries, rock the cradle, write, sing, dance, and BE! Think about society not just permitting but fostering and nurturing that spirit. Encourage, do we say? How about reckon, uphold, sanction, and embrace? Doesn't that sound like society on a good day?

Well, that's it, folks. society, breaking stereotypes, promoting equality, and encouraging female empowerment while we all bask in the warm glow of her sea-changing makeover. Are we dreaming? Perhaps. But a collective dream can become a new reality when shared and acted upon. After all, society is just our collective self, isn't it? Imagine the possibilities. Hence, until you do, stay sharp, stay empowered, and remember to challenge the status quo if it doesn't dance to your tune. Why not?

How to Make a Difference: Steps to Empower Black Women

Education and awareness are the dynamic duo that can bring about powerful change. Who doesn't love a little heart-to-heart deep dive into the societal issues facing Black women? As you wipe away your crocodile tears, remember that the goal here is to empower, so strap on those knowledge boots and let's get walking.

Education comes by various means: schools, seminars, workshops, books, or even a good old-fashioned conversation with someone knowledgeable. What's important is that we open our minds to the riveting chronicles of Black women's plights and accomplishments. After all, you can only progress if you know the starting point, right? So, take notes, folks, because awareness is a journey, and everyone loves an epic adventure.

Once we've got our educational game on point, it's time for mentorship and encouragement. The glitter sprinkled over the cake is empowerment. Black women need role models—people who've walked the walk and fought the fight, emerging as the queens they are. Not to replace the fairy godmother—who among us wouldn't want a magic wand? But having someone who can walk beside you, guide you, and live to tell the tale? That's real-life magic right there.

Mentors can also be the cheerleading squad for these strong Black women in the making, standing on the sidelines, chanting their names, and waiting until that perfect moment comes to dunk them in a cooler of confidence. The more encouragement and support they receive, the more resilient and capable they become in overcoming life's curveballs.

Now, let's discuss cultural competence—not as cool as a superpower, but still with the potential to save the day. We can define it as the ability to understand, respect, and interact constructively with people of diverse backgrounds. In simpler terms, it's having a good relationship with others and embracing the beauty of diversity. In today's global village, cultural competence is more than just a fancy skill to put on your résumé; it's understanding that, at times, you'll feel like a fish out of water, but you'll quickly learn how to swim.

So, what do we get when we blend education and awareness, mentorship, and encouragement with a heaping spoonful of cultural competence? It's the perfect recipe for empowering Black women. And trust me, this dish is more satisfying than devouring your mama's famous mac and cheese after a long day of fighting the good fight.

Weaving together these critical elements and seasoning them with our wit, humor, and knowledge about Black women's legacies will result in the perfect alchemy of empowerment. Our guests who pledged to pay tribute to Black women might end up gifting something more profound—the promise of a brighter future.

And so, with the white spaces strategically placed like well-placed pauses in a symphony, we travel through each vital talking point, leaving behind a trail of empowerment for Black women to pick up and wield as they embark on their journey to shape the future. After all, it is a tribute to Black women. Let's hope they can hold onto their crowns while wading through our sarcasm-strewn content.

Now go forth, keep reading, and always remember that it's not just about breaking the glass ceiling but also about patching up the cracks for the next generation. So let us wittingly empower Black women, create opportunities, and help open doors to new possibilities—all while sneaking in a laugh or two.

The obstacles Black women face are by no means a walk in the park, but darn it, they're pushing through (they didn't come this far to give up, right?). And their unwavering determination deserves recognition, applause, and a standing ovation from the world.

Speaking of the world, it's high time for a monumental and collective shift in societal views because Black women are here to stay and thrive if you haven't been paying attention. It's time to squash stereotypes, crush inequality, and fire up the engines of female empowerment as we race towards a world that respects and nurtures the legacies of Black women.

Educate yourself and others about the empowering legacies of Black women. Share their stories, their achievements, and their importance. Mentor a young Black girl and tell her how powerful and capable she is.

Today, we come together to celebrate the incredible legacy that each of you carries within. This is a testament to the enduring contributions of Black women throughout history. Your achievements, innovations, and the indelible impact you've made across various fields and movements have shaped the world we live in today.

As we delve into this celebration, it's not just about acknowledging the past but also about drawing inspiration for the generations that follow. Your stories, resilience, and triumphs become a wellspring of motivation for those who come after you. The mere knowledge of your journey lights up a path for others, showing them that the sky is not the limit—it's just the view.

But celebration alone is not enough; we must preserve these invaluable legacies. This section explores initiatives dedicated to documenting, preserving, and sharing the stories of Black women. It's about ensuring that your contributions are eternally woven into the fabric of history, leaving an indomitable mark for posterity.

Passing the torch of leadership is a vital act in this narrative. The torch you carry, fueled by the fire of your passion and determination, is not meant to be held by just one.

Your legacies continuously inspire the future we envision, and it's a future where Black women lead fearlessly, innovate boundlessly, and contribute limitlessly. This isn't just a chapter; it's a manifesto for a future that builds upon the foundations you've laid. A future where every Black woman is empowered to embrace her potential, knowing that she stands on the shoulders of giants.

So, here's to you, us, and the beautiful mosaic of strength, wisdom, and grace that Black women bring to the world. May this celebration fuel the flame of inspiration, preserve, and pass on the torch of leadership, and shape a future where your legacy is remembered and lived every day.

CHAPTER 10: EMBRACING RESILIENCE: A COMPREHENSIVE APPROACH TO ENHANCING MENTAL HEALTH AND WELL-BEING OF BLACK WOMEN

Now, why do we need to talk about this? Dr. Seuss didn't say, "Sometimes the questions are complicated, and the answers are simple," just for the heck of it. The issue of Black women's mental health is nothing short of a maze, but the importance of navigating it cannot be overstated.

Whether it's stretching a meager paycheck to cover the bills or tackling unwelcome micro-aggressions at the workplace, Black women have been juggling multiple hats like they're in a never-ending circus performance. And, well, all the while, they're also expected to live up to society's ever-changing parameters of what constitutes a "strong Black woman." No girl should ever wake up and think, "I am not white, skinny, and rich. Therefore, I am unworthy." I mean, come on! It's the end of 2023; can't we do better?

And then they wonder why serious discussions about Black women's mental health are necessary. It's like wondering why your plant is wilting when you've been watering it with soda.

But here's the tea. Mental health problems don't discriminate. I repeat, mental health issues don't give two hoots about who they latch onto. They're like that annoying, clingy ex who can't take a hint. However, when it comes to Black women, they're not just battling depression or anxiety. No, no. They've got to fight the hydra-headed monster of systemic racism, socioeconomic disparities, and cultural stigmatization all at once!

So, when we discuss Black women's mental health, trust me, we are not just opening a can of worms. We are staring down an army of bloodthirsty, saber-toothed tigers, and guess who's leading the charge? The potent weapon of resilience.

In this quest to empower Black women, let's highlight, examine, and break down the barriers affecting their mental health. Doing so lays the foundation for a more in-depth understanding and a united front to bring about essential change. Here's to the power of conversation, the resilience of Black women, and a future that says, "Not today" to mental health challenges.

And before we move on, can I say to all the Black women reading this: You are diamonds, and don't let anyone tell you otherwise!

Stigma and Mental Health

Stigma is that pesky little critter that clings to mental health like gum on a hot sidewalk. It's the reason Aunt Carol whispers, "She's... you know, seeing a therapist," as if disclosing a fondness for midnight graveyard picnics. And when it comes to Black women, oh honey, it's not just whispers; it's a cacophony of outdated judgments and head shakes.

Understanding Stigma? That's the appetizer on our seven-course menu of 'Let's Get Real.' Stigma is stealthy; it slips into the mind's back door, convincing you that mental health is a luxury suite where only the weak check in. It paints every therapy session with a shade of 'crazy' and dismisses medication as an overreaction. "Girl, you don't need a doctor; you just need to pray more," says the choir of misinformed parishioners. Bless their hearts.

Now, let me lay it down for you: Stigma is like that uninvited guest at the cookout who criticizes the mac 'n' cheese but eats two plates of it. It's this mindset that mental health is taboo, a no-go zone for strong, resilient Black women. Resilience is supposed to be our only shield against the slings and arrows of life's outrageous fortunes.

Stigma is fed a steady diet of ignorance, so it grows bigger and bolder, spreading from person to person faster than juicy gossip in a hair salon. "Did you hear about Sheryl?" becomes the theme song, and "Struggling Silently" is the dance everyone's doing.

But breathe easy because the effect of stigma on Black women's mental health is where the plot thickens, and we rally the troops. Imagine being in a battle where your armor is constantly questioned. "Are you sure you want to wear that to fight depression?" It looks kind of heavy." Sounds ridiculous, right? But that's what it's like. The suspicion that donning mental health armor is an overreaction only leaves one feeling more exposed.

Stigma whispers dangerous little lies like, "If you seek help, you'll be judged," creating a quagmire of self-doubt and fear. It guilt-trips you into believing that you're betraying the 'strong Black woman' archetype if you dare voice your troubles. It's as if your mental health passport has been stamped with a bold "DENIED" whenever you seek to travel to the land of self-care.

And can we talk about the workplace for a second? Stress is supposed to be your plus-one to every meeting because "you can manage it," and anxiety is perceived as a side-effect of ambition. The silent side-eye when you're perceived as the 'angry Black woman' for just having a bad day could power a small city with its intensity.

We're doing the Charleston on a tightrope, with stigma on one side and genuine mental health needs on the other. Slip too far into stigma, and you're a "basket case." Lean too heavily on expressing how you actually feel, and you're not "holding it together." It's the kind of dance that would make the Roaring Twenties blush.

So, amid the chuckles and head nods, let's not forget the real talk: Stigma is a bully, but it's a bully that can be silenced with knowledge, openness, and a willingness to swap judgment for empathy. It's about time we flip the script, stare down the stigma, and declare, "Not today, buddy. We're having none of your nonsense."

Black Women and Mental Health: Understanding the Scenario

Being a Black woman in America. Some days, it feels like being a superheroine without the cool spandex suit. "We've got the power of resilience, the force of endurance, and enough sass to make everyone around us do a double take," I chuckled, indulging in my usual mix of sarcasm and humor.

Located at the intersection of race and gender, Black women are dealing with a truckload of issues that can make a typical Tuesday feel like a Herculean trial. Racism, sexism, domestic violence, chronic stress—it's like they've won the lottery for problems (only it's a jackpot no one wishes to win). These pressing obstacles contribute to mental health disorders like anxiety, depression, and PTSD at rates higher than our fair counterparts. "You'd think we would at least get some kind of superhero allowance with all these challenges, right?" I quipped, hoping to lighten the mood of our deep dive.

Now, take your caffeine to the side as we look into the infamous socioeconomic factors. Ah, yes, the fond term is given to the many menacing interferences that impact Black women's mental health, like a nosy neighbor: poverty, education inequity, lack of access to quality healthcare, and income instability. Add racial discrimination in job markets and healthcare systems (yes, it's a thing) into the blender, press pulse, and voila! You've got the ultimate smoothie for mental health stressors.

Let's sprinkle some intersectionality into our rather grim smoothie. For those of you wondering what intersectionality is, it's like being stuck at a red traffic signal in all directions. Being Black, a woman, and sometimes from a low-income background means facing discrimination that's like a mega combo meal of societal biases. It's like entering a battle on three different fronts. The impact? A banquet of mental health issues that often go untreated due to the stigma and barriers to accessing mental health services.

So, while casually juggling overwhelming mental health issues and societal barriers, Black women navigate intersectionality like seasoned pros. And let me tell you, it's not as easy as turning the corner at a crossroads. It's a roundabout with no exit sign.

From dealing with social norms that dictate suppressing emotions to battling the 'strong Black woman' stereotype, which, by the way, does not earn us a Marvel film series deal, these fearsome warriors are striving to normalize mental health conversations one step at a time. They are fighting to move beyond what society tells them to be—"strong" and "silent"—to embrace an innovative plot twist, one where they seek help when needed and share their load.

After all, every superheroine needs a break to recharge their powers—a lesson hard learned by our Black women in their quest for mental well-being.

So, the next time you see a Black woman, don't just see her struggles. Instead, appreciate her intricate narrative, woven with persistence and resilience, and share in her laughter as she trots down the hard road of survival. Because, trust me, it takes more than a pinch of audacity and a dash of boldness to be a Black woman!

Coping Strategies and Adaptive Behaviors

Coping strategies and adaptive behaviors are the bread and butter of living in a world that seems to throw challenges at us relentlessly, like dodgeballs in P.E. class. For Black women, having effective coping strategies and adaptive behaviors is a bit like having a superhero cape, which is essential in navigating their unique challenges.

Firstly, let's address the relevance of coping strategies. Coping strategies are like spare tires; you hope to never have to use them, but when the need arises, you're grateful to have them. They are a set of go-to techniques that help us keep our heads above water in the sometimes-tumultuous sea of life. For Black women, building a repertoire of coping strategies is particularly essential to dealing with the triple threat of race, gender, and social-class-based stressors. Talk about juggling multiple chainsaws while standing on a tightrope, right?

Enter stage left, adaptive behaviors! The trusty sidekick to coping strategies helps ensure that they are effectively utilized. When the going gets tough, adaptive behaviors are what propel us through the challenges, keeping us on the path to success and sanity. Like wearing a funky hat on a bad hair day, adaptive behaviors make the best of a not-so-great situation. For Black women, learning and embracing adaptive behaviors means fostering resilience and arming themselves with valuable tools for surviving and thriving despite the cards they are dealt by society.

Let's talk about resilience, the power ingredient that ties everything together. Picture resilience as the magical glue that holds the pieces of the coping strategies-adaptive behaviors puzzle together. Resilience is the ability to bounce back from life's challenges and not just tolerate adversity but find ways to triumph over it. It's the cherry on top of the coping strategies and adaptive behavior sundae.

For Black women, resilience is both a necessity and a superpower. It's what allows them to rise above the hurdles that are unique to their experience and to come out on the other side with their mental health intact. They aren't just the queens of survival but also of thriving and growing, all while conquering the world as only they know how.

So, what have we learned? Coping strategies are the foundation for navigating life's challenges; adaptive behaviors help us maximize their effectiveness; and resilience is the powerhouse that makes it all possible.

As we spin our web of coping strategies and adaptive behaviors, let's not forget that each Black woman's journey is unique. So, while these tools and superpowers might save the day for Spiderwoman, Batwoman, or Wonder Woman, for the everyday Black woman, remember to customize and fine-tune these strategies to make them work for you. After all, being the superhero of your own life is what it's all about.

Empowering Black Women: Boosting Mental Health

Empowerment is that magical word that makes you feel like you can conquer the world! But empowerment is more than just a catchy buzzword; it's a pathway to improved mental health, especially for Black women. So, how exactly do we navigate this empowerment pathway for Black women?

One great way to start is by widening our lens to the wonderful world of community psychology. Imagine this: professionals in the field of psychology, but with superhero capes swooping in to empower Black women in their communities. Okay, not capes, but you get the picture. The role of community psychologists is essential in empowering Black women by working on strategies to reduce environmental stressors, increase access to resources and services, and facilitate their empowerment in society.

But let's pump the brakes for a second and address the elephant in the room—or, should I say, the "cultural competence" in the room. The importance of culturally sensitive counseling and therapy cannot be overstated. After all, understanding a person's cultural background adds a critical dimension to the therapeutic process. It's like adding a new flavor to your favorite ice cream—suddenly, everything makes sense (and tastes better, too).

Now, let's talk about the importance of culturally sensitive counseling, shall we? First, it helps bridge the gap between the psychologist and the client, promoting a sense of trust and understanding. Who wouldn't want to open up to someone who knows their cultural background? It's like having a conversation with a long-lost friend.

Furthermore, culturally sensitive counseling allows for a nuanced exploration of the unique experiences and challenges faced by Black women, making the therapy process much more effective. It's like getting a tailor-made suit instead of a one-size-fits-all—every little detail counts, right?

To sum up, empowering Black women through mental health initiatives involves utilizing the skills of community superheroes (I mean, psychologists) to create strategies for reducing stressors and increasing access to resources, all while delivering culturally sensitive counseling that hits home, like mom's home-cooked meals. And who wouldn't want a taste of that?

I know what you're thinking: "Great, we've got the tools, but what's next?" Wow, you're a fast learner, huh? The next step is weaving these strategies into policy interventions and community initiatives that support Black women individually and collectively. This way, we can help Black women overcome mental health challenges, thrive, and reach their full potential, because, after all, empowered Black women are a true force to be reckoned with.

So, let's embark on this journey toward improved mental health, celebrating the resilience and strength of Black women along the way. Because, at the end of the day, isn't that what empowerment is all about?

Policy Interventions and Community Initiatives

To put it tactfully, the world of policy-making is a glacially-paced, bureaucratic labyrinth of inefficiency, but don't let that depressing fact get you down! It's time we dive into the wonderful world of policy interventions and community initiatives because, trust me, I know a good time when I see one.

You see, Black women have some unique mental health challenges that can't be ignored, and we don't need mediocre policies that are as useful as a chocolate teapot. Stand back, ladies and gentlemen; let's push for policies that provide culturally sensitive mental health services and make healthcare accessible and affordable for everyone. I know, I know, it's revolutionary to believe that everyone should be able to afford mental health care, right?

Now, on to community-based efforts for mental health advocacy because, let's face it, sometimes a group of passionate, committed individuals makes a bigger impact than a hundred snoozing bureaucrats. Better grab your pom-poms; we're about to cheer on some grassroots change-makers!

Community organizations can play a vital role in challenging stigma and advocating for the mental health needs of Black women. Why wait for a knight in shining armor when a village of fabulous, independent women working together is much more empowering?

Collectively, they can identify gaps in mental health services, push for increased awareness, and provide support for Black women's rights in their own neighborhoods. You know what they say: if you want something done right, do it yourself (or with a team of fabulous, determined women).

Furthermore, these community efforts can encourage open conversations about mental health because the only thing more taboo than mental health in our society is talking about it. And let's face it, conversations as awkward as the one you have with your dentist, as they're elbow-deep in your mouth, are usually the most necessary.

So, there you have it—just a little glimpse of what policy interventions and community initiatives can bring to the table to improve Black women's mental health and well-being. Just remember, it's not all doom and gloom; there's plenty of room for humor, sarcasm, and a dash of fabulousness in the pursuit of mental health equality. One policy at a time, folks. And who said improving mental health couldn't be a quirky and hilarious path to empowerment?

We need to join forces and demand inclusive and culturally competent mental health treatments reinforced by supportive policy interventions and community-based initiatives.

So spread the word, plant the seeds of change, and watch the magnificent garden of well-being and resilience flourish. After all, as the great Maya Angelou once said, "You may not control all the events that happen to you, but you can decide not to be reduced by them."

CHAPTER 11: REDEFINING BEAUTY: EMBRACING AUTHENTICITY AND DIVERSITY IN HISTORIC AND FUTURE BLACK WOMEN'S BEAUTY IDEALS

Now, you must be bewildered. "What's this fuss about historical Black women's beauty ideals?" I can hear the skeptics. Well, beauty, as they say, has always been in the eye of the beholder, and the beholder has been, through history, wildly inconsistent.

Ancient Nubian queens were the pioneers and influencers sans Instagram. They defined beauty not with a glimpse of a mascara wand but by staying true to their natural persona. Celebrating their dark skin and kinky hair was the epitome of beauty. But as Oscar Wilde rightly mentioned, "No great artist ever sees things as they are." "If he did, he would cease to be an artist." With every generation, these ideals vibrated towards change.

"But why the importance of redefining beauty?" another question asks. You could continue living your life unaware of this transformation and still manage to Netflix and chill. But redefining beauty is like waking up to a new language of self-expression. It's about establishing a dialogue, not about why Elizabeth Taylor's angular face is beautiful.

Paving the way for this awakening is the call to diversity and authenticity. Such corporate-speak buzzwords these are! Are they swirling around every panel discussion or debate? But step back; diversity and authenticity in beauty ideals aren't some newly baked pie. They're the constant "Nagging Nancy" in the background, persistently striving for recognition in their domain.

Imagine a world where everyone resembles Barbie—a platinum blonde with a size waist. So boringly uniform, right? Luckily for us, humans come in vibrant shades of sizes, shapes, and colors. This diversity is our rich artistic palette that adorns our global story. This time, we have a beautiful Black canvas painting us a masterpiece instead of a white canvas.

On the other hand, authenticity is not a luxurious castle we must build but a shack we must rediscover within us. It asks us to hang up our pretentious veil and embrace the beauty in our imperfections, repeating the mantra, "Honey, this is me, and I am fabulous."

Now, you may be wondering, "Is this a beauty manifesto or a philosophical ramble?" It's a bit of both, to be honest. It's about sketching the silhouette of a confident 'woman of color' who stands tall in the mirror, basking in the glory of her natural beauty and rejoicing in every bit of the skin she lives in. And this ethos of diversity and authenticity, with a gentle tease of humor and sarcasm, is to unravel the journey of the often-overlooked subject—the quintessential beauty of Black women!

With redefined brushes of inclusivity and acceptance, the beauty narrative is finally moving beyond norms, setting a new course for a culturally diverse fairness meter where every woman can be her kind of beautiful. Are you ready for the journey? Besides, if you have to stand out in a sea of sameness, it always helps to redefine.

The Clay Vessel of History: Discovering Ancient Beauty

There was a time, long before the glitz and glam of Hollywood and centuries before #NoFilter selfies, when beauty was more than skin deep and went beyond the reach of Instagram's influence. Here's the thing: our African ancestors were the true trendsetters, with queens like Nefertiti and Cleopatra slaying the beauty game before beauty vlogs were even a thing.

Now, let's time travel to an era where African queens set beauty standards and having a fierce look didn't involve a YouTube tutorial. These regal ladies were the epitome of grace and allure, rocking bold and intricate hairstyles that would make any modern-day influencer bow down in respect. And their skin? Honey, let's say that their radiant natural complexions didn't require an arsenal of cosmetics or a 10-step Korean skincare routine. They owned the original 'I woke up like this' vibe with a confidence that was off the hieroglyphic charts.

In a time when the term 'exotic' hadn't been misappropriated by travel brochures, tribal body art and jewelry spoke volumes. Imagine walking into a room where ink, not your LinkedIn profile, told your life story. Tattoos, scarifications, and piercings weren't a Saturday night whim fueled by one too many cocktails but sacred symbols representing one's lineage, status, and accomplishments. Oh, and the bling? Who needs Tiffany's when you've got handcrafted jewelry that would shame any luxury designer's collection?

And about those hairdos—we're talking about a historic use of natural hair that would make any modern-day product junkie's collection look like child's play. Centuries before the term' big chop,' these women rocked locs, braids, and afros not just as hairstyles but as profound statements of identity, ones that said, 'I am connected to the earth, my ancestors, and my roots.' Let's not even start on the gravity-defying hair sculptures that would leave any contemporary stylist googling for a how-to guide.

All right, hit the brakes on this ancient African beauty train and park for a moment. Let's reflect on how every elegantly elongated neck, every dramatically lined eye, and every meticulously crafted bead strung on these women was an ode to their lineage and a bold dismissal of a one-size-fits-all beauty approach. And unlike today's digital age, where a new Instagram filter pops up weekly to tweak reality, these ladies kept it 100% real—authenticity was their default setting.

So, as we moonwalk back from our historical beauty catwalk, let's take a second to chuckle at the notion that these timeless beauty practices are having a 'moment' in our modern world. The nerve, right? Our ancestors are somewhere giving a side-eye to the concept of 'trends.' These beauty ideals weren't just fleeting hashtags; they were a lifestyle that celebrated diversity way before it was considered cool – talk about being avant-garde without even trying!

Remember, this magnificence wasn't about Yolo; it was about legacy, self-expression, and an undiluted sense of self that laughed in the face of any 'one-size-fits-all' beauty standard. So, let's tip our proverbial hats off to these women who didn't just follow beauty trends; they etched them into history with a boldness that still resonates to this day.

Reshaping Ideas: Transition Period

We're headed for the period where the beauty ideals of Black women took a detour. Colonialism, you sneaky little thing, you swept in with your large ships and fancy uniforms, but you forgot to pack your acceptance of diversity suitcase back in the West, did you?

Western colonialism—that's correct, folks. A non-refundable, business class ticket to change. A complimentary tag along with forced ideals and standards of beauty. At the flash of a musket, the ebony skin that mirrored the nights that bore tales of warriors and enchantresses was suddenly frowned upon. The curly locks defied gravity, told centuries' worth of stories, and became an object of ridicule. Beauty, reimagined under duress, entered its rebellious teenage years.

The new beauty phenomenon wasn't the high school crush you'd pine for. The African queens were no longer the prom queens. Bodacious curves were swapped for linear figures, and natural twists were traded for silkier counterparts. Let's not even broach the topic of skin-lightening. The beauty she once acknowledged in her reflection had been swapped with an alien, unwelcome, and forcibly imposed image. Vanity mirrors were transformed into funhouse mirrors devoid of laughter.

And just like any troublesome teenager, accepting these new standards didn't happen overnight. Embracing a beauty ideal that looked nothing like them? Well, even the sun doesn't rise in the West, does it? So, you see, this was not just a change made for the sake of change. It was a paradigm shift that broadened the beauty spectrum but simultaneously diluted the self-belief and self-pride of Black women.

But wait! Let's not descend into melancholy. Humor me a bit, please. Imagine forcing a giraffe to live among penguins and then criticizing it for sticking its neck out. Absurd indeed, right? This was a struggle layered with irony.

So, there you have it! The Transition Period, in all its glory, or lack thereof, was a time of change that left its mark, albeit a blemish, on Black beauty ideals. It was a grand theatrical show, per se, where the audience desperately awaited a twist in the story—the binding beauty code needed to be broken.

Black is Beautiful: Embracing Originality

In the kaleidoscopic world of beauty, where trends come and go faster than a catwalk model on a greased treadmill, a profound revolution has been strutting its stuff since the skies of societal norms started to scatter with clouds of change. Enter the 'Black is Beautiful' revolution, a rallying cry from the 1960s that's still echoing today because Black was, is, and always will be beautiful. This wasn't your average fad; it wasn't about swapping red lipstick for coral shades. It was, and remains, a seismic shift in the very bedrock of beauty ideals.

So, there you have it! The Transition Period, in all its glory, or lack thereof, it was a time of change that left its mark, albeit a blemish, on Black beauty ideals. It was a grand theatrical show, per se, where the audience desperately awaited a twist in the story—the binding beauty code needed to be broken.

And who led this charge? Oh, just a few courageous luminaries who evidently missed the memo that said they should conform to unrealistic beauty standards. Let's tip our hats to icons like Diana Ross, who didn't just exit stage left; she strutted, hair flowing, voice soaring, boldly embodying the elegance and grandeur of Black beauty. Over in a smoky jazz bar, you might spot Nina Simone hypnotizing the room with her soulful voice, unapologetic radiance, and signature style.

Fast forward, and this salvo of original Black beauty didn't just spark a trend; it ignited an unstoppable blaze. And lest we forget, towering figures like Grace Jones and, later on, the queen of everything, Oprah Winfrey, didn't just walk into the room; they owned it. They dismantled the very foundations of the established beauty norms with every photo shoot and public appearance, piecing them back together into a mural that portrayed real, diverse beauty.

This was no superficial scratching at the surface of the behemoth of beauty standards. Nope, the 'Black is Beautiful' movement was the bulldozer and the jackhammer—a cultural upheaval of how beauty was projected and perceived. It wasn't just about accepting Black beauty but about celebrating it loudly, proudly, and on Broadway billboards.

The movement thrust diversity into the limelight, not as a sidekick or an afterthought but as the main attraction. Thanks to this shift, Black children could finally see themselves as the superheroes and princesses of their own stories, no longer relegated to longing for resemblances in a world that offered them little representation.

As this cultural renaissance weaved its way through the fashion runways, music videos, and Hollywood blockbusters, it was clear this wasn't another trend you could wave off like that aunt at family reunions who won't stop talking about her cats. The 'Black is Beautiful' rebellion had one simple yet profound message: Black beauty isn't an alternative; it's a vibrant and permanent fixture on the beauty scene.

But as they say in show business, "What's next?" After this dalliance with authentic Black glory, there's an air of expectancy—a collective holding of breath, waiting to see if this enthralling narrative of Black beauty will continue to rewrite the script, turning centuries of exclusivity into burgeoning tales of inclusivity. As the media and pop culture canvas expands, Black beauty ideals no longer lurk beneath the heavy drapes of history but step confidently into the light. They lead the way, showing us all that the future of beauty is here, it's real, and it's not going anywhere.

Today's Beauty Spectrum: Being Unapologetically Beautiful

Who needs those beauty magazines dictating rigid standards when you've got your mesmerizing, unmistakable reflections smiling back at you in the mirror? Didn't get an invitation to the diversity party? Today's beauty industry is throwing open its doors, shouting loudly and clearly, "Everyone is invited."

Diversity—once a decorative word on corporate vision statements—is now shaping the very foundations of the beauty industry. I bet you didn't see that coming! The intoxicating mix of various skin tones, exclusive features, eclectic styles, and, yes, "all sizes matter" is what characterizes the beauty landscape today. It's like going to a potluck dinner where everyone brings their most fabulous dishes—the result? A rich, inclusive banquet where there's something delicious for everyone!

Front and center of this 'throw open the doors' scenario are the feisty trailblazers of the natural hair movement. They dare to defy the tyranny of the straightening irons, saying a big "Au Revoir" to the repressive reign of chemical relaxers. It's time for twist-outs, Bantu knots, and Afros to claim the throne. Hear that, world? That's the sound of the hair quake that's shaking the very roots of the beauty industry—the final rebellion against straight-hair supremacy. Ladies, be prepared to embrace your spirals, glaciers, and killer kinks—the curls are coming and mean business!

Beauty today isn't a mold to be filled, but a masterpiece bursting through generations of stereotypes and the stuffy vaults of societal expectations. It's an echo of strength, etched into our skin and bodies, a silent hymn passed down generation after generation, with each verse refined and melody enriched. Feel the rhythm, listen to its language—beauty is universal, transcending barriers—we are all invited, expected, and embraced.

After all, the world is a gigantic palette of diverse colors and varied textures. And let's face it, what's a panorama without a rainbow of colors? Isn't it high time we celebrated the spectrum of our beauty, from ebony to porcelain and everything in between?

For all those skeptics and naysayers still lurking around, pondering on the taglines of 'flawed perfection' saturated in the undercurrents of this seismic shift in beauty standards, decode this and decode it well: Beauty is now synonymous with authenticity. And why shouldn't it be? Aren't we tired of the cookie-cutter molds of fairness creams and silicone heroes?

So, here's to celebrating your own kind of beauty, no matter its shape or hue. Because, in the end, it's all about being unapologetically you.

Isn't diversity a party where the monotonous walls are pulled down and the doors thrown open to an exhilarating symphony of varied voices and unique experiences? Where the only agenda is to celebrate the beautiful myriad of hues we are? And trust me, it's a party you wouldn't want to miss.

Tomorrow's Canvas: Progressing Towards an Inclusive Future

Well, if we're to sail on this boat called "Inclusive Future," we ought to vet who's steering, right? Are we looking at a fly-by-night trend that'll drop diversity like a hot potato when it's no longer 'cool,' or is there a genuine shift sparking from the roots?

Gladly, my pretties, beauty diversity isn't giving us those unhealthy fling vibes. This baby's here to stay. Fads, you see, usually run out of fuel faster than a guy runs from commitment after proclaiming love on the second date. Diversity, on the other hand, is like that hard-to-get lover. It took its time to allure us, and now that it has, it isn't going anywhere anytime soon.

But hey, "talk is cheap," as that notorious ex of mine used to say. So, let's fetch some proof.

Open your Instagram feed and behold the army of robust beauties proudly flaunting kinky curls and radiant dark skin, cheerfully dismantling rigid, stereotypical standards. They aren't fleeting visitors; they're settlers! Permanent settlers added their flavors of beauty to this once monoculture soil.

However, just like you can't master the art of a flawless smokey eye after watching one YouTube tutorial, acceptance of varied beauty definitions hasn't been a cakewalk. That's where education and advocacy have been absolute game-changers.

It's not about 'dictating' what beauty should look like but 'educating' that beauty, like Baskin Robbins' array of delights, comes in a plethora of flavors. The more we understand and embrace this, the easier we can wave a heartfelt goodbye to beauty biases.

But don't let your guard down just yet. The road to this utopian beauty world is still under construction, peppered with potholes of ignorance that we need to fill. In this pursuit, advocates have been our superheroes without capes, voicing for inclusive beauty standards and challenging contrived stereotypes.

So, what rainbow are we chasing at the end of this struggle?

Picture this: A world where beauty aisles flaunt Afro-hair products as proudly as blonde ones. In a world where 'beige' isn't the default nude, billboards are sprinkled with as many dark-skinned models as fair ones. That's a sight for sore eyes, isn't it?

Hold on to your wigs, ladies! A future that sees us whooping in celebration of our diversity isn't a pie in the sky any longer. We're smelling the dawn of a new era, a behemoth wheel-turn of beauty ideals, favoring every color on the palette. The journey towards this future isn't a ramp walk in stilettos, but who said beauty comes easy?

So, as we tread forward to make this vision a gorgeous reality, I say, get yourself together and be ready to watch the grand show where standard beauty ideals are shredded and the spotlight is passed onto the rightful—all of us!

And guess what? There's no VIP section here. Every size, every shade, and every texture shares front-row seats because, at last, it's not a world taking beauty cues from a select few. It's a world where beauty is as unique and original as our fingerprints. Welcome aboard this beautiful rollercoaster ride, folks! More twists and turns are on the way.

And 'fad'? It can flirt with some other inferior revolution. We're into something serious here!

From ancient queens to modern screen sirens, Black women have striven to redefine beauty and embrace authenticity in an ever-changing world.

Each step of the way, these wonderful, spicy game-changers have laid the groundwork for today's diversity and representation party. So why does this even matter, you ask? Come on, think about it for half a second: authenticity and diversity aren't just colorful cupcakes at an inclusive party; they're the ingredients that make us who we are—unique and beautiful in our own right.

As we throw confetti in the air and celebrate the unyielding spirit of Black women who've played a major part in redefining beauty norms (I mean, would you look at that gorgeous hair? Let's not forget the road that brought us here. The struggle, triumphs, and resilience led to the celebration of all shapes and hues.

So, let's raise a toast to the transformed landscapes of beauty ideals and to the pioneers who insist on unapologetic self-expression in all its curly, brown-skinned glory! Because, honestly, where would the world be without a little #BlackGirlMagic?

Remember, progress in the beauty industry is not just something to be observed; it's a colorful palette that deserves to be embraced. After all, life's too short to stick to monochrome, don't you think?

CHAPTER 12: CHAMPIONS OF CHANGE: CELEBRATING THE TRAILBLAZING ACHIEVEMENTS OF BLACK WOMEN IN SPORTS

Oh! Where to begin with the sublime saga of Black women leaping, quite literally, out of bounds into the sporting chronicles? If you haven't heard their stories, sit tight, because you are in for a riveting ride. How apt is it that these vibrant, robust, and relentless women obliterating records and shattering stereotypes brought our blah, monotonous world to life? Say hello to the champions you didn't know you needed.

All this glitz and glam didn't come without its fair share of roadblocks. These women have always had to fight an uphill battle, refusing to break in the face of what I like to call a double whammy—overcoming the hurdles of both race and gender discrimination. I mean, isn't life exciting enough? You see, not only did they have to prove their worth as athletes, but they also had to do so while challenging the stereotypical notions of race and gender spun by centuries of misconceptions.

Let me paint you a pretty (or not-so-pretty) picture. Picture booze-swigging, cigar-puffing, balding men snickering at a lady attempting to hit a ball. Imagine that lady being a Black woman in a largely pale-skinned arena. Our heroes, these Black sporting divas, graciously tiptoed (or maybe stomped) around these obstacles, chucking them aside like an old bag of chips (because who needs that extra load?).

It's riotous to think that in a world where the fastest man is a Black man, women of the same descent had to fight tooth and nail for representation, credit, and validation in the sports dome. And boy, did they rise to the occasion like a tidal wave at the shore! Unapologetic, unabashed, and unstoppable, these ladies defied norms, broke through ceilings, and somehow still found time to sashay down the street, making heads turn.

From Alice Coachman dusting the dirt off her shoulders and becoming the first Black woman to bag an Olympic gold on foreign soil to Althea Gibson smashing the Whites-only shackles of international tennis. These stories are anything but ordinary.

Forgotten names, unfamiliar faces, triumphant tales. It's about time the world knew, appreciated, and celebrated their awe-inspiring achievements.

Trailblazing the Olympic Fields

My, oh, my! Have we got an epic tale to tell, a story that twines itself around two mighty forces—the world's most prestigious games and the relentless zeal of Black women? We're diving into the realm of the Olympics—a land littered with the shattered remains of 'can't do it' messages and littered with records that turn yesterday's impossible into today's breakfast.

And amidst this crowd, who are the ones flipping those gender and racial scripts? Well, it's the Black women athletes. While the Olympic Games have been a long-standing tradition, their recognition of everyone—and we mean everyone—was a tad late. But let's forget about that part; we'll bill it as "Even Olympic games go through awkward puberty." But when they finally opened their arms (or, should we say, fields) to Black women, wow! The world got a taste of a different level of sporting prowess.

Enough is said about everyone. Let's finally throw the spotlight where it's owed. Louise Stokes and Tidye Pickett. Who are they? Only the courageous duo who took on the double-headed monster of racial and gender prejudice bashed their heads and ran all the way to the 1932 Olympics. Did I forget to mention it? They were the first Black women to do so.

Louise Stokes, the faster-than-average-lightning sprinter, was denied the chance to compete in the 1932 Olympics, not due to a lack of skill but because of 1932! Yet, despite being put on what we'll call an "unfair extended bench," Louise didn't let that deter her Olympic dreams because, let's face it, once an athlete, she always had a heart of steel. She came back, sprinting her way to the subsequent Olympics, too.

Then there's our second hero, Tidye Pickett, who pushed boundaries in a very literal sense by making waves in the field of hurdles. Despite facing numerous obstacles (pun intended), both on and off the track, she climbed over them (see what I did there?) and carved her name in the annals of Olympic history, not just once but twice!

That being said, it's not all rosy and free of hurdles. Navigating through the Olympic Games was like playing an insane level of Temple Run, filled with prejudiced monsters and biased beasts. But these trailblazers showed the world that when you have goals bigger than the barriers, you only leave behind your footprint, and records.

In an alternate universe where there were no racial or gender biases, one can only imagine the medals they would have bagged! They ran their races, jumped their hurdles, and smashed through barriers not just on the track but in the hearts and minds of millions across the world. Now, isn't that more precious than a chunk of gold with five interlocking rings?

Remember their names because, when you sketch the history of the Olympics, Louise Stokes and Tidye Pickett are the ones who laid the ink. And like the legend Usain Bolt once said, "Records are made to be broken." And so, the story continues. Our champion ladies shall keep lighting the trail with every stride and record they break.

The Queens of the Courts

Permit me to take you on a journey into the world of tennis and basketball, where a few trailblazing Black women single-handedly (or, should I say, double-handedly?) changed the face of these sports. Yes, I'm talking about none other than Ora Washington, Althea Gibson, Lynette Woodard, and Cheryl Miller.

Step into my time machine as we head back to when Ora Washington casually established herself as the Queen of Tennis. Ms. Washington, who ruled tennis and basketball courts during the 1930s and '40s, has won seventy-four (!) Amateur Athletic Union (AAU) titles in both sports. I mean, if you want a multi-talented game-changer, look no further. And then there's Althea Gibson, the original Serena Williams. This incredible woman broke multiple color barriers and became the first Black athlete to win a Grand Slam—yes, a Grand Slam—winning the French Open in 1956. Not stopping there, Althea went on to grab Wimbledon and U.S. Open titles as well! Talk about shaking the sports world to its core!

Now, closing our tennis chapter, let's dribble onto the basketball courts, where Lynette Woodard and Cheryl Miller are making history. These ladies didn't just play with the boys; they smashed through any glass backboards in their path. Lynette Woodard, an Olympic gold medalist (that's right, gold), was the first woman to ever play for the famous Harlem Globetrotters.

What's even more noteworthy is that Lynette didn't just stop there; she went on to build a concrete foundation for women in basketball by becoming the women's basketball coach and athletic director at her alma mater, the University of Kansas. Woodard is living proof that basketball (or any sport, for that matter) has no gender boundaries.

Now, Cheryl Miller, where do I even begin? A nickname like "Reggie's sister" doesn't stick unless you're a basketball prodigy or a sibling of NBA legend Reggie Miller. Cheryl Miller didn't just break records; she shattered them into a million pieces and set them on fire. With two NCAA championships under her belt and a record for most points scored in a single game (105, if you can believe it), she also went on to represent the U.S. basketball team and win an Olympic gold medal in 1984.

After all these explosive on-court achievements, Queen Miller decided it was time to sprinkle some of that magic off-court—she became the first female analyst to call a nationally televised NBA game. When you thought Cheryl had no more championships in her, she proved everyone wrong as she coached her way into a WNIT championship and two NCAA tournaments as the head coach of the USC Trojans. We might as well rename her "Cheryl' Mic Drop' Miller."

The unapologetic, unstoppable force of four Black women who flaunted their athletic prowess shattered racial and gender barriers and taught the world that anyone, regardless of race or gender, could excel in the competitive arenas of tennis and basketball. I'd say it's time for a standing ovation! Oh yes, and don't forget to thank them for continually raising the bar for future generations of athletes.

Ice and Track Showdown: Stories of Debi Thomas, Jackie Joyner-Kersee and 'Flo-Jo'

Sliding and sprinting through history with some of the most remarkable women who broke records and shattered glass ceilings with the elegance of a pirouette and the speed of a gazelle. We've already high-fived the likes of tennis titans and basketball legends, and now it's time to glide over the ice and dash down the tracks with

Debi Thomas, Jackie Joyner-Kersee, and the 'fastest woman of all time,' Miss Flo-Jo herself.

Let's start with Debi Thomas, shall we? Imagine being so absurdly talented that you can say, "Why yes, I am an Olympic medalist and a surgeon; thanks for asking!" That's Debi for you—a figure skating prodigy with the finesse of an artist and the focus of a brain surgeon, quite literally. She glided her way into our hearts and the Olympic podium in 1988, becoming the first African American to nab a medal at the Winter Olympics in figure skating. Debi danced on the ice better than most of us can walk on solid ground, and with each jump and spin, she carved a narrative far more impactful than her skate marks on the rink.

Now, if Debi's story had you jumping with joy, brace yourself for the dynamic duo of the tracks, Jackie Joyner-Kersee, and Florence Griffith Joyner, known to fans as 'Flo-Jo.' Jackie took multitasking to Olympian levels; she didn't just win gold medals in both the heptathlon and the long jump; she decided to be the best there ever was. She scoffed at the idea of limitations and leaped her way to three Olympic gold medals, one silver, and two bronze, becoming the most decorated female athlete in track and field history. And let's not forget to mention her world record in the heptathlon. "Jackie, who?" said nobody, ever.

And then there was Flo-Jo, the woman whose speed was only matched by her flamboyant one-legged race suits and fierce nails. "Wind resistance?" she laughed, as she probably kicked up a breeze that could power a small town. Florence Griffith Joyner dazzled the world at the 1988 Seoul Olympics with her 100m and 200m sprints, and let's face it, her style was as iconic as her stride. Earning the title 'fastest woman of all time,' she served us glam and gold in equal measure, proving that femininity and athleticism go together like peanut butter and jelly, or, in Flo-Jo terms, like sparkle and speed.

So, what do these awe-inspiring women have in common besides their obvious athletic prowess and a collection of shiny baubles known as Olympic medals? They mastered the art of excellence with every slice of their skates and every stride of their spikes. It wasn't just about setting records but about resetting the narrative for Black women in sports. They were not here merely to participate; they came, they saw, and they conquered, all while carving out a space for those to come.

Their legacies serve as a reminder that no matter how cold the ice may be or how hard the track, with a dash of audacity, some killer threads, and a whole lot of talent, records, and barriers are there for the taking—or breaking. The baton has been passed; the ice has smoothed over for the next daring dreamer who looks up at these stars and thinks, "Heck, why not me?"

And to the skeptics who still murmur that a woman's place is not on the podium or the front page of the sports section, we salute you with a chuckle, because clearly, you need to pay attention. These women have already left you in the dust—the ice shavings and track rubber—ages ago.

A New Era: The Invincible Williams and the Bionic Biles

The Williams sisters are the dynamic duo that took tennis by storm and never looked back! Venus and Serena Williams have been the talk of the tennis world since they first stepped onto the court, boasting an astonishing number of titles, and making the rest of us feel inadequate in the process.

The sisters' powerful serves, jaw-dropping prowess, and unbeatable (on most days) teamwork truly put the "sibling" in "sibling rivalry." Their combined Grand Slam titles could fill an Olympic-sized swimming pool (not literally, but you get the point), and still, they show no signs of slowing down.

From their hair-whipping moments on the green to their unabashed love of fashion, the Williams sisters have redefined what being a Black woman in sports means. Despite facing obstacles and discrimination, they have emerged as an inspiring symbol of strength and resilience that has left the world in awe.

Now, brace yourselves as we get gymnastic. The world of cartwheels and backflips has never seen the likes of Gabby Douglas and Simone Biles! Say "ta-da" to two trailblazers who continue to prove that reaching new heights is possible (quite literally).

Gabby Douglas, dubbed the "Flying Squirrel," took home two Olympic gold medals back in 2012, becoming the first African American in Olympic history to win the individual all-around champion title. Her gravity-defying flips, combined with her unwavering determination, resonate deeply with the hearts of millions, making her a true role model in every sense of the word.

But wait, there's more! Enter Simone Biles, a force of nature whose numerous gold medals simply can't be contemplated without your head spinning. Biles has dominated gymnastics with a unique blend of power, finesse, and gravity-defying skills, earning her the well-deserved nickname "The Bionic Woman." Rumor has it that she was born with springs in her legs, but that's yet to be confirmed.

Owning a staggering 19 World Championship titles and 4 Olympic golds, Biles has redefined the realm of possibility in gymnastics. But it's not just her athletic feats that inspire—it's her unfiltered personality and openness in discussing pertinent issues like mental health that make her an authentic, relatable role model for young athletes everywhere.

These four phenomenal women have broken records and shattered stereotypes and expectations. As Venus, Serena, Gabby, and Simone continue dominating their respective sports, they leave a legacy that inspires future generations of Black female athletes. Each triumph in the face of adversity symbolizes Black women's unwavering resilience and ability to change the game. And let's face it, they've made sweating look good.

So, the next time you're in your living room trying to imitate Serena's unstoppable backhand or attempting to do a backflip à la Gabby (please don't try this at home, folks), remember the remarkable journey of these Black trailblazers who have paved the way, and the profound impact they have made not only in the world of sports but also in inspiring a new generation to believe that anything is possible.

From Where We Stand Now: A Look into Today's Black Women in Sports

Sports is that magical realm where we unite, grind, sweat, and, more often than not, either get gloriously victorious or heartbreakingly close. And when it comes to contemporary Black athletes, let's just say they are rewriting history, and how! They're like those cool kids in class who make records for a hobby.

You might have heard of a certain Simone Biles, the gravity-defying, four-time Olympic gold medalist with 19 World Championship gold medals. Rumor has it that they're replacing the term "awesome" in dictionaries with "Simone Biles."

Then there's Shelly-Ann Fraser-Pryce. They call her the fastest woman on the planet; I say even The Flash has a poster of her in his room. She's a bolt from the blues, four times over!

Taking a detour to basketball, if we don't talk about Maya Moore, we'll be on the 'foul' side of things. We are talking about a behemoth who won practically every trophy out there—from World Championships to the Olympics. Then, just like a telenovela plot twist, she hit pause on her career to pursue justice for a wrongfully convicted man. She nailed it and came back to the game with double glory. Now, isn't that a plot for a Hollywood flick?

But, my dear sports-loving friend, remember the yin to this yang. With every jaw-dropping leap and lightning-fast sprint, there's an underbelly of struggle against racial and gender prejudice. We don't need to time-travel; it's right here in the Century of Woke.

Take Caster Semenya, for instance. An athlete par excellence is the target of arguably the most controversial ruling—the gender testing regulations. It's almost like the authorities thought, "Why not add a dash of discrimination to our daily dose of espresso, eh?"

Or let's talk about Serena Williams. No, not about her formidable 23 Grand Slam singles titles; that's passé. Instead, she fights against sexist dress code rules and the scrutiny surrounding her "emotion" after a loss. The more things change, folks, the more they stay the same—sports, life, you name it.

These women are playing on the court and fighting off it, juggling with a sort of finesse that should give them extra points. They are honing their skills on the battlefield of sport while also schooling us in the art of smashing prejudice and wearing courage.

So, these ladies aren't just toppling tennis balls and shattering glass ceilings but also taking a head-on tackle against racial and gender inequality. They are winning while bringing about change, one record and one prejudiced mentality at a time. It's like running a marathon while simultaneously doing salsa.

The next time you put on your sneakers or tune in to a game, remember that for these athletes, it is not merely about winning. It's about demolishing biases, squashing stereotypes, and changing the rules of the game. After all, who needs a mere game point when you can score a point for humanity?

So, here's to these champions of change, celebrating their victories on and off the field! They're certainly not just playing the game;

they're revising the rulebook with each winning shot! Now that's Athletics 101 for real!

The persistence, determination, exceptional talent, and sheer guts of these phenomenal women are not just awe-inspiring little bedtime stories but, more significantly, charters of change in the big, bad world of sports.

Each triumph was a hand firmly planted on the sticky web of gender and racial prejudice, ripping it apart one win at a time. Their stories signify an era of revolution, spawned not just by athletic prowess but also by their nerve and tenacity. Much like a game of dominoes, each successful stride amplified the cause, paving the way for the next generation of athletes.

CHAPTER 13: AMPLIFYING VOICES, DRIVING CHANGE: THE RESILIENCE AND INFLUENCE OF BLACK WOMEN IN POLITICS

Nothing says 'backbone of society' like resilient Black women who've played a significant role in the political sphere. Oh! Did you think political influence was an all-boys club?

It's crucial to remember that Black women haven't had it easy. Picture Atlas shouldering the weight of splendid resilience, having faced the standard female battles and the layered complexity of racial prejudice. Yet, they've moved mountains—or, should we say, policies—with their ceaseless efforts and indomitable spirit.

Black women in politics are like that essential spice, driving change where it matters most, and boy! have they stirred the salad. They've been here, making history and ensuring the future gets the memo about 'the utterly fabulous force called Black women.'

As they say, "When things get tough, the tough get going." Amidst chuckles and puzzlement, let's march forward, acknowledging these genuine gladiators in the arena of politics. Their contributions have been etched into the annals of history, and we will be gushing about them.

Trailblazing Black Women in Politics

First on the list is Shirley Chisholm. Oh, "Unbought and Unbossed," as her campaign slogan proclaimed, and trust me, she was anything but sugary sweet. When I say trailblazing, this woman invented the term. She didn't just push boundaries; she bulldozed them. Becoming the first African American woman in Congress in 1968, she took a sledgehammer to the ceiling when, in 1972, she announced her bid for the presidency. She may not have won, but she shook the entrenched norms! Put on your sunglasses, folks, because that ceiling now reflects some serious sunlight.

The next person is Barbara Jordan. With a voice that could command your attention and a charm that could demand your respect, if you thought politics was no place for a Black woman, Ms. Jordan was ready to correct your misconceptions. In Texas, she pulled a fast one on prejudice when she became the first Southern African-American woman elected to the U.S. House of

Representatives in 1972. She didn't just participate in the Watergate hearings, folks; she made them an opportunity to give the nation a soul shake.

Now, the last person on the list is Carol Moseley Braun. She looked at the glass ceiling and then looked back at Shirley Chisholm, probably shrugging, and said, "Let's do this!" If you think navigating the political corridors of power is tough, try doing it as the first-ever Black woman senator. Yes, this fabulous woman claimed that honor in 1992, and trust me, she owned that chamber like she was born for it, advocating for education and women's rights and calling out Confederate insignia on federal flags, all while rocking some stylish signature neck scarves.

Here's the thing. These women were not just mavericks with audacity; they were navigators, lighting the way for future generations. Do you think the political arena is a battleground now? Imagine being a Black woman in times when the phrase "civil rights" would cause a stir at a dinner table. The story may be a bit bitter, but the aftertaste—the legacy of an invitation to equality and representation—is somewhat sweeter than the sweetest southern pecan pie.

Contemporary Black Women in Politics

In the cruelly stratified kingdom of American politics, a groundbreaking quartet of dynamic Black women dared to challenge the status quo, their stars illuminating the path for others to follow. Let's call these magnificently defiant women "The Fearless Four."

Maxine Waters, referred to as Auntie Maxine by her legion of admirers, has served in Congress longer than One Direction has been alive. Quick on her feet and sharper than a double-edged sword, she has turned the political arena into her own concert, where she plays the symphony of justice and equality. With her inherent gift of setting social media and the House floor ablaze simultaneously, Waters has spent decades advocating for the rights of economic minorities. Seasoned with experience but not marinated in complacency, she's fighting battles at the age when most of us would be watching Netflix and forgetting where we kept the remote.

Then there's Kamala Harris, who doesn't just crack glass ceilings but shatters them to smithereens! With her complex cultural background reflecting the very diversity America prides itself on, she sashayed into the White House as the first female Vice President, leaving her haters and the patriarchy quaking in their boots. Harris, who often has the phrase "groundbreaking first" attached to her like moss to a rock, personifies empowerment and not just promises change but acts on it.

The rest of the Fab Four are no less extraordinary. Stacey Abrams is like the much-awaited plot twist in your favorite TV show. The kind that has you dropping your popcorn in surprise as she almost single-handedly turned Georgia blue. A voting rights activist and the backbone of many political victories, Abrams radiates the sort of calm tenacity one needs when upturning long-standing political biases. She is a master at debunking myths about impossibilities. Time and time again, Abrams shows us that "impossible" means "I'm possible."

Completing the quartet is Ayanna Pressley, a woman who can probably win an arm-wrestling match against adversity. She refuses to be a background character in the story of America, instead choosing to become its pivotal protagonist. Losing her hair to alopecia didn't steal her thunder; it revealed the storm within her. As the first Black woman elected to Congress from Massachusetts, Pressley embodies each of the three F's: fierce, fearless, and fabulous!

These four incredible women aren't just involved in politics. They are reshaping, repackaging, and serving it on a platter for future generations to feast upon. They're not just politicians. They're game-changers, and, dare I say it, absolute rockstars!

Black women in politics are like Beyoncé songs: powerful, memorable, and universally loved (well, almost universally). But unlike Beyonce's songs, they are still not heard often enough. So, no, they won't put a ring on it.' Instead, they'll pull up a chair, sit at the table of politics, and make their presence known, one law, one bylaw, and one Twitter clapback at a time.

Organizations Focused on Black Women's Political Empowerment

Higher Heights is this revolutionary organization that's been shaking things up and amplifying the voices of Black women in the political sphere. Run solely by Black women, for Black women, they've been working tirelessly to increase Black women's representation and influence in politics. And let me tell you, they're doing a fantastic job. They cook up some beautiful projects like #BlackWomenLead, which is not related to cooking and is about encouraging Black women to take seats in political office.

Let's dish some sweet tea on the Black Women's Roundtable. This spicy little collective isn't messing around. They're a national women's civil rights organization that doesn't only have a killer name but a killer mission. This roundtable is a group of fierce, fierce women who provide an 'interactive' policy. They're stirring up change and serving a warm cup of empowerment, equity, and positive social change. Trust me; you don't want to spill this tea.

And the celebration of girl power doesn't stop there. Enter the National Organization of Black Elected Legislative Women (NOBEL). Can we take a moment to appreciate that powerful acronym? Talk about 'Nobel' indeed. These wonderful women are on a roll, like hot butter on a breakfast muffin. They're passionately addressing the incredibly low representation of African American women within the ranks of elected officials. They're committed to increasing and promoting the presence of Black women in government roles. Just like Black Panther did for the superhero world, they're doing it for the political world—pioneering, inspirational, and empowering.

These organizations are working their magic to rewrite the narrative for Black women in politics. And to all the aspiring Black women leaders out there, remember, as Michelle Obama once said, "There's no magic to achievement." It's really about hard work, choices, and persistence." So, get out there and make a difference. After all, if not us, who? If not now, when? Or, if you prefer, in the immortal words of the ever-so-delightful Mary Poppins, "Well begun is half done."

So, here's a toast to every Black woman making a mark in the political world. To those dazzling regal queens jousting with words in courts, governing states, leading causes, and bossing it up in the still predominantly male world of politics, we salute you! And to those yet to come, remember, you are the dreams of a thousand slaves—brave, powerful, and resilient.

The Role of Black Women's Political Activism

All hail the queens of political activism! No, we're not talking about bra-burning, tie-dye-wearing, placard-holding activist stereotypes. We're talking about those who are playing chess while others are playing checkers. They strategically navigate the complicated realms of civil rights and politics without flinching. These ladies have guts, galls, and glory that last a lifetime!

Let's start with Maggie Mitchell, Margaret Mitchell, for formal introductions. Margaret, however, had no time for formalities. This fiery soul was one of the founders of the NAACP, and her weapon of choice? A typewriter, and boy, did she know how to arm it! She was like a wordsmith ninja, spinning stories and weaving narratives that championed equality and justice and escalated the plight of the African-American community into the national consciousness. And you thought your 10th-grade writing assignment was hard; it is, but doesn't it feel like a walk in the park now?

Next up, if you crossed Diane Nash in a dark alley, would you be scared? No, you would not, because she'd probably be singing "Freedom's name is mighty sweet" from her Freedom Rider days. But don't let the song fool you! Nash was a linchpin in the Civil Rights Movement, leading student sit-ins and Freedom Rides and facing down Southern prejudice with her Northern resilience. Her actions were instrumental in the desegregation of Southern establishments, openly challenging societal norms while subtly giving a slap to segregation policies right from Nashville to Mississippi. Talk about integrating with style!

Oh, I see you've met Bree Newsome. Except you don't shake hands with Newsome; you shake her hand while she's perched atop a flagpole, removing a Confederate flag in South Carolina. And while we're here, a quick pop quiz: how many of us have climbed a 30-foot flagpole? Yeah, I thought so! She was arrested for her actions but made a resounding statement: that symbols of hate had no place in society. It's like when you remove that ugly gnome from your neighbor's front yard, with more legal consequences and national attention. And a gnome probably doesn't represent systemic racism.

Mitchell, Nash, and Newsome—each of these women—is a testament to the courage and determination that come along when everything is on the line. They show us that activism isn't an overnight T-shirt sale but dedicating one's life to justice and equality. It comes from standing up, stepping in, and sometimes from stepping onto a flagpole.

Remember folks! Red Bull does not sponsor these strong Black women; their courage comes from a steadfast resolve for societal change. They checkmate discrimination and bigotry.

Barriers Faced by Black Women in Politics

The heated pool of politics isn't the cheeriest place to be, and when you're a Black woman, it can sometimes feel like swimming through a sea of molasses. It's sticky, challenging, and almost impossible, but the effects ripple across the entire surface when you swing your arms around.

If you thought dealing with discrimination was bad enough, try handling intersectional discrimination—the un-fun house where race, gender, and class discrimination all intertwine into a nightmarish labyrinth of prejudice. It sounds like a party I wouldn't want to attend! But say no more; let the courage of Black women speak for themselves, who, faced with such obstacles, have gotten creative with their resilience, granting themselves an uncanny knack for doing the impossible and turning lemony discrimination into lemonade.

The political sphere, my friends, is not the most welcoming place for Black women. It's a bit like turning up to a fancy dress party only to realize you're the only one who got the memo about dressing up. The lack of representation of Black women in politics is, let's say, 'outstanding' and not in a good way. But who wants to be part of a club that doesn't want them? Except in this case, being part of the 'club' means making changes that affect billions—no biggie.

With all of a Black woman politician's might, knowledge, and capability, societal stereotypes come into play like an uninvited party pooper, who's supposed to be dictating policy? No, how about we downplay your role in how you look, tone, and even your hair? Let's not forget the old chestnut, "You're too emotional or aggressive." Have people met politicians before?

This isn't your regular old meet-cute story between a woman and the world of politics; it's a thriller filled with suspense—will she, won't she, oh wait, she did it! And it ends like any good story should, with our resilient heroines refusing to see obstacles as barriers but more as fences. And fences, as any good rebel would tell you, are made to be climbed over, tunneled under, or, in some extreme but necessary cases, smashed right down.

So, instead of standing back and watching these fantastic women battle the storm alone, why not throw them a lifeline or two? Not out of sympathy—puh-lease, they're way too skilled and determined to need that—but just in recognition of a fabulous pool party thrown by Black women in politics.

Strategies for Supporting and Encouraging Black Women in Politics

Resilient, powerful, and fearless. Black women in politics. It was quite a feat. Their voices echo through the hallowed halls of government institutions, challenging the status quo and shouting, "We need change!" So, how can we support and encourage Black women in politics?

First, recognize and value their voices. You see, merely hearing is not enough; we need to actually listen, learn, and amplify. It's something like turning up the volume on your favorite track. Dr. Martin Luther King Jr. once said, "Our lives begin to end the day we become silent about things that matter." And trust me, diversity in political representation truly matters. So, let's not unplug the stereo when the beat of progress starts playing. Let's not turn a blind eye, or rather a deaf ear, to the struggle and accomplishments of Black women in politics.

And speaking of achievements, they rarely come alone. Behind the spotlight, a helping hand and mentorship play a significant role. Be it a Today's Show style makeover or teaching them the ins and outs of cunning political maneuvers (which goes beyond just knowing how to word a witty tweet perfectly).

But wait, let's not forget that this isn't charity poker, where everyone gets dealt the same hand. Not everyone is dealt a fair hand from the get-go. So, it's time for a new player at the table, "equal opportunity." We need to fund and invest in Black female candidates. Just imagine that your investment could lead to the next Michelle Obama dropping the mic on political inequalities. It's kind of like investing in Microsoft in the early eighties; you see the potential, and you know it's going to shake the world—well, in this case, the political spectrum!

Now, here is where we come in, folks! Promoting diversity and inclusion is important because having only one shade of color in the crayon box will not create a vibrant masterpiece. Recognize the power and necessity of their voices because every opinion matters. Encourage an inclusive political ecosystem that is ripe for Black women to thrive in. A rainbow makes for a more beautiful sight.

And before you start thinking of assembling an Avengers-style team of powerful Black politicians, remember, it's not about getting your name etched on the Infinity Gauntlet of social justice champions (though that does have a nice ring, won't you agree?). It's about standing up for the truth, like a rebellion against an unjust empire.

Do you want to level up your activism game? Great! Start by recognizing and valuing the voices of Black women. Pawn your inherent biases at the door and step into inclusive spaces where diverse voices are welcomed and appreciated.

And with that, you have geared up for the journey towards empowering Black women in politics! But hush! Let's not pat ourselves on the back just yet. There's still so much work to be done. In the battle for equality, remember, 'winter is always coming,' and the fight is over once justice is served. So, keep that sword of support and shield of encouragement handy as we bravely march forward.

Throughout history, and certainly in the times we find ourselves in today, Black women have shown that they are not just seat fillers in the political arena. They are champions leading the way to bring policies that seek justice and equality for all, not just the privileged few.

The likes of Kamala Harris, Stacey Abrams, and Ayanna Pressley are not just names that will end up in textbooks. They are women who continue to fight for justice and equality, carving paths through the dense forest of the political landscape. They are not just survivors but game-changers, resilient as cockroaches in a nuclear war. Their groundbreaking work lays the groundwork for future politicians of color, reinforcing the belief that they can lead and make a difference.

Paying tribute to these women is like trying to sum up the Game of Thrones series in a tweet—nearly impossible because of their profound influence and resilience. These women maneuver through the political landscape like ballet dancers gracefully power through Swan Lake—with dedication, strength, and sheer force of will. They've tackled every barrier thrown in their path like a professional NFL player, and let me tell you, it's been no child's play.

But their influence extends far beyond the political sphere. They inspire young Black girls to dream beyond the stars, to aspire for positions of power and influence, and to work towards a world where one's race doesn't dictate their opportunities.

In the eternal words of Beyonce, 'Who runs the world? Girls!' But after this deep dive, I'd like to propose a tiny amendment. 'Who runs the world? Black women!' So, here's to the Black women of the past, present, and future, who continue to stand tall against all odds, beating drums of change and 'twisting' the narrative for themselves and future generations. Because this isn't a fairy tale, there aren't any glass slippers, just sturdy combat boots, paving the way for a brighter, more inclusive future.

CHAPTER 14: BALANCING ACTS: THE QUEST FOR ECONOMIC STABILITY AMIDST THE INEQUITY FACED BY BLACK WOMEN

An elusive phantom that seems to disappear every time it is approached. It's like trying to find a parking spot on a busy Saturday or the missing sock from your last laundry load. But less mundane and a whole heap more significant.

Let's board our way-back machine for a brief encounter with history. Or may I call it 'herstory,' primarily because it's all about 'her,' the Black woman, and also because it's a neat play on words that I found incredibly hard to resist. Anyone who objects to this linguistic indulgence can forward their complaints to the nonexistent box of 'Stuff I Couldn't Care Less About.' Right next to the missing socks.

Once upon a dreadful time, our heroines made an involuntary entry into the workforce as forced enslaved laborers. Yes, folks, the same roles were conveniently excluded from the "Respectable Professions" list. Fast forward a few centuries, and they are faced with the arduous task of dismantling walls of gender and racial expectations in workplaces. What's worse is dealing with the doubt of those who can't believe they actually want job advancement opportunities. They expected Black women to be content with running the 100-meter race with a 50-meter handicap.

Now you might be wondering: Why the fuzz about economic equity for Black women? Well, I was hoping you'd ask! The answer makes as much sense as pouring milk into your cereal bowl before the cereal itself. You see, Black women have long been the unsung heroines of our economy, tackling over-concentration in low-paying jobs and costly caregiving responsibilities. Yet, like an overworked intern, their contributions often need to be noticed and undervalued. Nothing shouts 'irony' more than society's dependence on Black women to fulfill vital roles, then throwing them a wage gap broad enough to swallow their economic stability whole!

The situation is as frustrating as untangling the wires of your earphones and as heartbreaking as stepping on a Lego. But none of this is accidental; it's the equivalent of creating a game, setting the rules, and then deciding to be the referee as well. We're looking at you, white supremacy, and sexism.

So, next time you push that shopping cart, remember you're not just buying products but indirectly validating a system that can afford to pay less to the cashier, who's probably a Black woman—starting a fight for economic equity. Now, there's a cause you can add to your cart.

Inequitable Wages

It's no secret that pay scales are like a seesaw. Unfortunately, it's an imbalanced kind. For Black women, the financial seesaw has historically been cocked way down on the unfair side. Yes, way down! It's the end of 2023, and we're still talking about it. Doesn't that reek of progress?

The Census Bureau data says that as of 2019, Black women earned just 61.4 cents for every dollar earned by White non-Hispanic men. It's blindingly obvious that we're not just dealing with a "gap" anymore. It's more of a gulf, frankly speaking. Just don't get me started on the comparison with their counterparts from 'other' races and genders. Those numbers would make a grown man cry—if the grown man was interested in fairness, that is!

Now, you must be thinking, "But why is the wage gap still there?" Glad you asked! Player one: enter "Discrimination." This sly fox has always had an "invite-only" party in the wage brigade, and guess what? Black women never made it to the list!

Next in line, we have occupational segregation. That's a fancy way of saying that Black women, given their limited access to education and opportunities, end up mostly in low-wage, low-growth jobs. It's like being stuck in a nightmare where the alarm never goes off. Bid farewell to dreams of growing salaries, ladies!

Isn't it heartwarming to learn about systemic bias and lack of opportunity? It brings a tear to your eye, doesn't it? Oh, wait! We aren't done yet. Let's serve the icing on the catastrophe cake—the impact on Black women and their families. Another striking revelation for the curious among you: poverty isn't a picnic! It affects everything, from the quality of education to access to healthcare and the ability to save for a rainy day. Isn't that just the cherry on top of an already precarious life sundae?

And I mean, who needs savings anyway? It's just money. It's not like it's used for living expenses and emergencies, right? If you could cut the sarcasm with a knife, we would have enough to make a stylish cutlery set by now!

Employment Barriers

So, there we are, minding our own business, when suddenly, bam! The whopping elephant in the room is also known as workplace discrimination. "But wait!" you might interject, "Isn't that stuff against the law?" In a world governed by rainbows and unicorns, yes. But let's face it, we're not there yet.

Discrimination and biases against Black women burrow underground, infiltrating the workplace like pesky moles in a lawn. They are tricky beggars, often sneaky and implicit, making them harder to spot and challenge. These underhanded tactics feed off stereotypes, like biases about Black women's skills and work ethic, and unspoken, antiquated expectations about their supposed 'workplace roles.' Just imagine the audacity!

And here's the kicker. This discrimination often piles on a full plate, wherein access to education and job training programs is scarcer than hen's teeth. Not because Black women aren't hungry to learn or that they're unable to excel. But, more often than not, such opportunities are tucked away behind a curtain woven from systemic racism and the remnants of socioeconomic inequity. It's like looking for a needle in a haystack that was never there!

Then, the year 2020 stomped in, swinging the COVID-19 pandemic like a wrecking ball. A double whammy! The pandemic didn't just expose the neglected groundwork of our economic system; it paraded it around in technicolor! For Black women, the challenges thickened like plotlines in a soap opera. With a disproportionate number of Black women in frontline roles like healthcare, retail, and personal care, the pandemic wasn't just an abstract menace. It was a potential nightly dinner guest!

And while the rest of us grumbled about stale banana bread and sourdough starters, many Black women faced the daunting roulette of virus exposure at work. With insufficient occupational safety measures and a paycheck that suspiciously failed to match the risk involved, it was like being offered a donut with half the cream and twice the holes as everyone else's!

There you have it! A sneak peek into the storeroom of

employment barriers for Black women. It's a set of challenges that would make anyone quiver like jelly at a Zumba class. The concerning part? This isn't the plot of the latest dystopian novel. It's a reel of real-life struggles that Black women grapple with regularly, buried under uncanny resilience and quiet perseverance.

Unpaid Labor and Caregiving Responsibilities

The age-old question of balancing work and family while simultaneously performing the high-wire act of unpaid caregiving. For Black women, this question takes on a whole new level of complexity. With their innate ability to juggle multiple responsibilities, it's no wonder that Black women are often called "super sheroes" but even super sheroes need a helping hand now and then.

The caregiving burden on Black women is immense, as they often carry the weight of caring for both their immediate and extended families. With Auntie's hip surgery recovery this week, baby cousin's daycare pick-up, and Grandma's weekly doctor appointments, it's no wonder many Black women have perfected the art of appearing in two places at once. But, surely enough, even they know teleportation isn't a feasible career path.

While dispensing super shero-level caregiving, Black women also navigate the tightrope of working a full-time job (or two) to provide financial stability for their families. The sheer amount of energy and attention they devote to unpaid caregiving is likely beyond the wildest dreams of any company offering "unlimited" vacation days.

But fear not! We're in the 21st century, and there have got to be solutions to support Black women in their dual roles, right? Let's peek into the magical world of potential solutions that could alleviate this seemingly impossible burden.

First on the list is accessible and affordable childcare. This would likely be at the top if Black women had a genie to grant one wish (or even three wishes). By implementing policies and programs that provide financial support for childcare expenses, we allow Black women to focus on their careers without struggling to find someone to watch the kids.

Next up: flexible work schedules. Gone are the days when everyone was expected to clock in at 9 a.m. and clock out at 5 p.m.

sharp. Employers need to provide genuine flexibility in working hours and location so Black women can create the work schedules that best suit their unique caregiving needs. Let's not forget that working from home is no longer that distant utopia we once dared to dream about!

Last but certainly not least: paid family and personal leave. Imagine a world where Black women can take time off work without fear of losing their job or income to care for their loved ones, tend to personal health issues, or even just recharge their super shero batteries. Providing comprehensive paid family leave policies not only supports Black women in their unpaid caregiving responsibilities but also fosters a more equitable and inclusive work environment all around.

If you've been daydreaming about teleportation or calling an intergalactic super-shero hotline for help, let's take a step back into reality. Yes, the above solutions seem to represent that perfect, carefree world we all dream about. Still, they are viable proposals with immense potential to improve many lives, including Black women.

By recognizing and addressing Black women's unique and pressing challenges in balancing work and family while shouldering unpaid caregiving responsibilities, our society can work together to provide essential support systems. It's time to shine a well-deserved spotlight on the super sheroes in our lives and, in turn, create a world that ensures their well-being and success.

So, let's roll out the red carpet and pay tribute to the strength and resilience of Black women, championing them with the transformative change and action they truly deserve. After all, even super sheroes need a sidekick to help them save the day.

Addressing Housing and Transportation Inequality

The sweet life of economic stability is a distant dream for many, particularly for Black women. Housing and transportation, two critical elements for a stable life, are plagued with segregation and discrimination that disproportionately affect this demographic. Like an epic game of whack-a-mole, Black women face inequalities at every turn, making the quest for economic stability much like a never-ending quest in a twisted RPG game.

The economic impact of housing and transportation-based inequity goes far beyond having a roof over one's head or catching the morning bus. Like being stuck in a recurring nightmare loop, these disparities are deeply interconnected with employment opportunities, financial stability, access to education, and overall well-being. When Black women are unfairly ghettoized or limited to underfunded, underserved areas, they might as well be playing economic Jenga with the unstable base that is housing and transportation inequity.

But fear not, for super sheroes, also known as policymakers, activists, and changemakers, are working tirelessly to devise policies and measures to ensure equal access to housing and transportation. A utopian dream, you say. Nay, the power of zoning reforms, fair housing law enforcement, investments in transportation infrastructure, and targeted affordable housing initiatives can slowly but surely bridge the chasm of inequity. All it takes is some persistence, concerted effort, and perhaps a sprinkle of pixie dust (or maybe more federal and state funding, but hey, pixie dust doesn't hurt, right?).

How do these dots connect, you wonder? Quality housing situated close to efficient transportation options paves the way for Black women to access better job opportunities and build wealth. When every piece of the puzzle fits seamlessly, Black women can break through systemic barriers and open the metaphorical door for future generations.

Empowering Black women to achieve economic stability is a sumptuous meal served best with adequate housing and transportation options, spiced with a pinch of sarcasm and a dash of humor. Though the challenges they face are no laughing matter, appreciating Black women's gritty determination and spirit is key to unlocking a more equitable, downright fabulous future.

So, take a moment to bask in the glory of Black women's resilience, and let us collectively create a world where the quest for economic stability becomes achievable for everyone—like endless loopholes, sinister traps, and dramatic sound effects.

Empowering Black Women Entrepreneurs

If you're a Black woman looking forward to running your own

business, don't fret! You're about to enter the ring with the other gladiator businesspeople. Wait, does that sound like an 80's video game? To be honest, your challenging journey might be more exciting.

Below are some of the challenges that are as common to Black women entrepreneurs as traffic on a Monday morning.

Firstly, access to capital. These three words could probably be featured as the main villain in 'The Chronicles of the Black Women Entrepreneurs.' No, this is not about a movie script but about an unfortunate reality. While money doesn't grow on trees, it may as well be buried six feet under for Black women entrepreneurs. Studies have shown reduced access to funding, which amounts to an average of merely 36% of what white male counterparts raise. This practically feels like trying to purchase a Gucci bag at a flea market price.

Oh, wait! Do we have a partner-in-crime for our main villain? Yes, we do—lack of resources. These are not just physical resources we're referring to but also intangible ones such as mentorship, networks, and opportunities—the sort of stuff that might not seem important until you're in the jungle without a map, compass, or even a genie from which to ask directions.

But let's hit pause on the gloom and doom scenario. Black women entrepreneurs have the potential to create, innovate, and inspire regardless of the hurdles. All they need is someone pointing in the right direction; we're here to do just that.

Let's think of boosting access to capital as playing 'Counter-Strike'—you got to know where the weapons are. Taking advantage of government grants, loans, and accelerator programs designed for minorities is a great start. But what good is a weapon if you don't know how to use it? That's where resources kick in! Knowledge-sharing platforms, entrepreneur networking, and mentorship programs can transform our 'Counter-Strike' novice into an expert player.

Now, despite the wicked witch and her evil consorts, our heroines—the Black women entrepreneurs—get to the game's final stage: 'Opportunities for Growth.' Put a pin in staff meetings, market expansion, and scaling operations for a moment. Let's talk about real growth, which comes from sharing experiences, learning from one another, and building communities that uplift each other. With the right support, let's just say we'll have more Oprah's in this world than we could count.

So, dear aspiring Black women entrepreneurs, remember that the success of your business isn't just about the profit margins but also about paving the way for future Black women entrepreneurs to slip into your loafers. Who knows, your local bakery could be the next Fortune 500!

Pathways Toward Lasting Economic Stability

Well, well! After wading through a sea of startling statistics and heart-rending realities, here we are. Anchored on the shore of 'Pathways toward Lasting Economic Stability.' Let me tell you straight out of the gate: the journey here was no pleasure cruise. And for our Black women, it's hardly been a luxury liner kind of experience. But this is where we set sail on the sturdy ship of solutions and strategies.

Education and professional development "Knowledge is power," they say, and clearly, whoever 'they' are wasn't bluffing. Because of our Black women, education has often proven to be a formidable ally in the fight for economic security. But wait, do you feel that breeze? It's the chilly wind of systemic obstacles and less-than-ideal socioeconomic backgrounds. So, while education and training are crucial, they remain a challenging catch for many because of an unfair ballgame. Whether it's community initiatives, financial aid opportunities, or upskilling programs, it is time to invest more in our Black women's educational journeys.

Mentorship and networking Just as every ship needs a compass to navigate, Black women need mentors to guide them and networking opportunities to create constructive connections. So why are such resources rarer than me turning down chocolate cake at a buffet? Are our Black women destined to sail into economic stability in the dead of night with no stars to guide them? Surely not! It's high time institutions, organizations, and communities hoisted the sail of inclusivity, amplifying networks that specifically support Black women.

Creating a more equitable work environment is a journey without a clear destination. But that isn't an excuse not to start the engine or, even worse, put on the reverse gear (yes, I'm looking at you, big corporate companies!). We need structural changes like equitable pay, family-friendly policies, and the cessation of gender and race bias. While we're at it, let's fast-track promotions for qualified Black women languishing in the corner cubicle and offer training and upskilling opportunities.

And there you have it—our roadmap to economic stability for Black women. Although, keep in mind, it isn't a joyride or weekend road trip. It's a long, arduous journey, but with perseverance and commitment, we can tune up the engine of opportunity and race down the highway to success. We've got the directions; now, all that's left is to put the pedal to the metal!

In the famous words of Rihanna, it's time to "Work, Work, Work, Work, Work!" But also, "pay, pay, pay, pay, pay" and "support, support, support, support, support!" Because our Black women have been giving their all for centuries, and it's about time we gave back.

Addressing the economic inequity faced by Black women is of utmost importance. Just think about it: if Ripley could single-handedly defeat an alien queen, imagine what an entire army of incredible Black women could accomplish! But seriously, by addressing these disparities, we'll be paving the way for a more equitable society where every individual can truly thrive. After all, economic stability plays a crucial role in breaking the vicious cycle of poverty and injustice.

Now, onto creating lasting change. As enticing as it may be to play the role of a lone hero, this issue demands collective power! Each of us has a part to play in this symphony of change—consumers, employers, policymakers, and God forbid, even politicians! The forces of good must unite to ensure that our workplaces are diverse, our pay is equitable, and opportunities are accessible. Yes, together, we play our role in bringing about more powerful change than the spells of ten thousand wizards combined!

We must join forces to pay an incredible tribute to Black women through transformative change and action. Because creating a brighter future for Black women is about more than just helping a few individuals. It's about creating a more just and equitable world for future generations.

So, let us keep faith in our ability to create a world where economic stability and justice for Black women are no longer just words spoken in hushed whispers. Let's make them a reality, a tangible force that allows each and every Black woman to thrive and unlock her full potential.

CHAPTER 15: CULTURAL PRESERVATION: GUARDIANS OF TRADITIONS AND IDENTITIES OF BLACK WOMEN

Cultural preservation is important, like that faithful cup of coffee every morning, sometimes overlooked but undeniably crucial. So, breathe in the rich aroma of our heritage, steeped in the brewing pot of history, and gathered, preserved, and passed on by those wonderful wizards we call Black women.

A cultural landmark isn't a static 'museum piece,' not just a fading photograph of grandmothers wearing traditional African headwraps. Cultural preservation is vibrant and fluid, like that dress you can't stop twirling in. It's the way we talk and cook, in the rhythm our bodies naturally sway to. And honey, Black women have long been guardians, master weavers, and often, the fabric upon which this rich mosaic of culture and identity exists.

Think about your grandma's kitchen smells, those African prints you flaunt, the humoral tunes in your ears, or even the pick-me-up rituals passed down through generations. Notice something common? Yes, these bear the distinct stamp of the cultural Midas, the Black woman.

You might raise an eyebrow and ask, "Why is this tribute specifically to Black women?" Highlighting the resilience and contributions of Black women isn't just a checklist activity; it's a neon sign in the face of history that often skated around their undeniable influence.

Historical Role of Black Women in Preserving Culture

Black women have been the unheralded sentinels of cultural preservation, staunchly standing guard over traditions and identities that have wiggled free from the clutches of time, colonialism, and, oh yes, gentrification. Can you even imagine such a job? It's like being asked to guard a technicolor unicorn—they're majestic but slip through your fingers if you blink.

Back in traditional African societies where cutting-edge utilities like Netflix were yet to be invented (oh, the horror), the role of Black women in cultural preservation shone brighter than my uncle's balding head at a solar eclipse gathering. Mother Earth could take a day off because these women were relentless nurturers, using storytelling, music, dance, and other art forms to weave the air with stories of their wisdom and beliefs. So, while it seems Mr. Hemingway and Ms. Rowling were the literati lights in cultural conservation, the plain truth is that the Black tribal woman spinning stories under the baobab was the unsung bard keeping her heritage alive. Indeed, as they memorably say, a library burns to the ground when an old person dies.

Fast forward to the years of slavery, where Black women's cultural identities were as welcome as a grenade at a peace conference. This was where the gallant gatekeepers of heritage were test-fried in oil hotter than Kim Kardashian's Instagram clicks. Yet they doggedly preserved their cultural identities like precious pearls tucked neatly within the oyster shells of their spirits. Whether it was the spirituals humming hope into their hearts or the secret symphony of their language, they had mastered the art of hiding cultural treasures in plain sight.

You see, it wasn't a battle of arms but of art, and who knew this better than the Black women? Much like Banksy in a Victorian gown, they were graffitiing culture across the blank canvas of penal existence. Slavery ended but armed with a paintbrush and a palette of heritage hues, these freedom fighters did not hang up their boots. They trudged on with bull-headed determination, chewing down capitalistic caution tapes and reclaiming the peace-laden pastures of their individual and collective identities.

In the vicissitudes of time, their preservation strategies have transformed into ingenious art forms, almost like Batman morphing into Batwoman! They might have hidden their cultural practices under cowrie shell-stitched quilts and soul-nourishing recipes during slavery, but now they've put them on display in museums, run cultural centers, and even championed policy changes. It's time the world napped its colonial hangover and acknowledged the seminal role of Black women in preserving culture and securing identities. They are not just guardians of traditions and identities; they are platforms for cultural dialogue, bridges over racial dividers, and authentic voices narrating the saga of their heritage.

So, next time you read a poem or a bestselling novel by a Black woman, don't pause at the literary merit. Look beneath the words, between the lines, and there will stand a proud Black woman, narrating a saga that has traveled from the wilderness of Africa, taking a jarring detour through the heart-wrenching lanes of slavery, and yet standing triumphantly in the modern era, weaving a vibrant mosaic of the past, the present, and the future of a race that refused to mute its identity against the din of cultural imperialism because that's a long story waiting to be told.

If you're wondering, I'm not applying for a poetic license. I'm just humbly attempting to present the gigantic portrait of Black women's tenacity in preserving culture, which otherwise fits uncomfortably into the minimalistic frames of academia. After all, as they say, culture is the identity that you can't take off after a stylish soiree. It's like a stubborn tattoo, and in the case of Black women, one that they have fiercely defended and devilishly displayed to the world. As they say, "Honey, if you got it, flaunt it!"

Black Women in Literature

Cultural preservation is like that one aunt, you know, the one who always insists on telling all those distant family stories at reunions that embarrass you as a teenager but somehow start to make sense as you become an adult. That's Black women for you in the sphere of literature. They're the custodians of the past, present, and future all at once, knitting together a colorful mosaic of African heritage through their compelling narratives.

Let's take a trip down memory lane, back to our high school literature class, and you'll remember the name Maya Angelou dancing around in your textbooks. I mean, who can forget the poignant words of "I Know Why the Caged Bird Sings," emblematically highlighting the struggles and victories of Black women throughout history? Likewise, playwright and Nobel laureate Toni Morrison and her work "Beloved" steeped themselves in rich themes of segregation, slavery, and sass. Ah! That's right, I said sass. Because if there's one thing these women knew how to do, it was telling their stories laced with courage, elegance, and an undeniable air of sass.

While we have our beloved authors, it would be a literary sacrilege to overlook the immense contribution of Black female poets. Hastings Banda said, "From the echoes of the past, the rumblings of the present, and the blueprints of the future, you can't separate our people from our poetry." And he was right! Echoing the sentiment, we find ourselves in the powerful verses of Phillis Wheatley, who, despite her colonial American enslavement, emerged as one of the revolutionary poets spearheading themes of Black identity. So, from poetry to powerful narratives, Black women have artistically danced on the stage of conniving tragedies and triumphs, presenting a colorful melting pot of cultural identity.

Now, if you think Black women just used literature as a storytelling tool, darling, you're wrong. Pardon my directness, but they didn't just use literature; they owned it! The level of individualism their works depict is equivalent to the Byzantine mosaic of their stories. You can't separate Black women from their literature, period. Their works were (and still are) a microscope, highlighting the many facets of Black womanhood.

From phrases that make your heart cry to paragraphs that make a smirk creep up your face, the art of storytelling by Black women isn't bound by the rules of logic. It totally defies Einstein's theory of relativity because, in their literary universe, the speed of light is not the limit; their words are. So, dust off those reading glasses and immerse yourself in this literary world. By exploring their works, you will not only gain a perceptive understanding of a culture, but you might also be induced by the indomitable spirit of resilience these Black women have mastered. Be warned, though, it's infectious! Embrace these literary masterpieces with an open mind and witness how beautifully Black women have preserved their cultural heritage through the written word—a heritage that's ripe with stories of independence, individuality, and, most importantly, an unwavering pride in being a Black woman. Let's appreciate these phenomenal women who have envisioned, written, and danced through the mosaic of time, preserving their heritage with every word they inked.

The Power of Music and Dance

Would Aretha Franklin and Bob Marley stand linguistic interpretations, or would Selena sway on Tejano tunes without these indomitable women? Oh, think again. These songbird warriors rescued their rich musical heritage from the jaws of obscurity and introduced the world to the delightful, soul-stirring music of Africa and the African diaspora. From Bessie Smith's empowered blues through Miriam Makeba's honest narratives to Rihanna's blending of contemporary sounds with Caribbean riffs, the sounds of these women have been the heartbeats of their culture, redefining genres and breaking records one melody at a time.

The music these women have created and graced tells a story of struggle, celebration, heartbreak, and liberation, rooted in Africa's rich soil, and spread to its scattered seeds in the diaspora. Jazz, blues, reggae, hip-hop—you name it, they have molded it. Heck, they've not just shaped it; they've owned it!

And, oh, how can I forget the dance floor? It's said that if actions speak louder than words, dance is a rock concert. Just like a rhythmic language infused with poignant storytelling, African and African diaspora dance styles have been visceral expressions of their intricate culture and traditions.

Black women have led the pack from the rhythmic stamp of Zulu warriors to the wriggle of the Samba, from the aesthetic twirls of ballet to the 'Bad & Boujee' twerks. Dance has been their canvas and limbs—the brush that colors life's joys, sorrows, struggles, and triumphs. Their choreographies, marked by powerful movement and celebratory spirit, have echoed, resonated, and preserved their cultural narratives for centuries.

Now, you'd think, with all these serenades and swaying's, we're nearing the part where cultural expression and preservation elope and live happily ever after, right? Well, not so fast! This is not a fairytale, folks; this is the real deal—the heroic story of Black women preserving their tradition and identity. And trust me, they've fought mighty wars with their harmonic and rhythmic arsenals.

In our world's grand opera, Black women have been the prima donnas, singing the arias of their cultures and swaying to their tunes like a balletic swan. Their voices have been their pens, dance, parchment, writing, and rewriting cultural history through melody and movement.

Wouldn't you agree that music isn't just a pastime but a passport, granting access to the hearts of cultures? And dance isn't just a physical art but the very lifeline of cultural expression and preservation. So, come along, folks, lend your ears to their music and sway to their rhythm as we dive headlong into our next stop—Visual Arts, Fashion, and Hair, the unsung heroes in the arena of cultural preservation. Look sharp, for they say beauty is in the eye of the beholder!

Visual Arts, Fashion, and Hair

Visual arts is like painting; it's just pushing pigment around on a canvas, right? WRONG! There's a lot more to it than that, especially when it comes to the impact of Black women in the world of visual arts. These masters of brush and canvas have been hard at work for centuries, infused with the spirit of our ancestors, creating powerful and evocative pieces that both honor and challenge our cultural heritage. Artists like Kara Walker, Faith Ringgold, and Mickalene Thomas (to name just a few names) have disrupted the art game with their fierce talent and unique perspectives, leaving an indelible mark on the ever-evolving world of visual arts.

Now, let's shift our focus from the canvas to the runway. Have you ever noticed the African influence in fashion? If not, you're either blind or living under a fashion-less rock. Seriously though, African patterns and designs have been taking over the world (yes, that's right), all thanks to the Black queens, designers, and fashionistas who said, "Hey, world! Look at our people's fashion's vibrant and stunning artistry, and try not to drool all over yourselves!" Designers like Duro Olowu, Maki Oh, and Grace Wales Bonner have been serving looks with an unapologetic African flair, turning heads everywhere, and making us all proud of the rich heritage we bring to the world of fashion. Trust me, you haven't lived until you've worn African print with confidence and the attitude of a boss.

Oh, and don't get me started on hair! I don't know if you've noticed, but hair is like a whole universe in itself, and we Black women are queens of that universe. Our crowns of curled, coiled, and braided glory have been speaking volumes (literally) about our cultural heritage since, well, forever. From traditional styles like cornrows and afros to modern twists like Bantu knots and locs, our hair empowers us and allows us to carry our ancestors on our very scalps. Have you ever seen a Black woman walk into a room and just own it with her fabulous, gravity-defying mane? It's a sight to behold, my friends.

Our hair has such a powerful presence that people just can't seem to keep their hands off it. But please, permit me to grace your life with an important life lesson: Thou shalt not touch the hair without permission. That's right—as arresting as our curls may be, it's not an open invitation for you to cop a feel. Just sit back, admire, and marvel at the power of our way back when hairstyles made a comeback and represented our culture on all our beautiful heads.

Community Leadership and Advocacy

These resilient Black women have not been content with merely being part of the crowd. Instead, they have indelibly impacted society while celebrating and preserving their cultural roots. Their journey is nothing short of a blockbuster movie packed with equal measures of trials, triumph, grit, and grace.

Let's pull the curtain back and venture into this exhilarating drama, shall we? The leading ladies in our narrative are none other than the phenomenal Black women who took on the reins of leadership, sparked changes, and left impressions that would endure for centuries. They do it all while sporting their cultural heritage like an eternal crown of glory. Talk about multifaceted!

These women aren't just champions of their community but custodians of their heritage. They understand the worth of a culture as diverse as the hues on an artist's palette and have been tempered in the crucible of history. They have maintained the narrative through inclusive museums, or, as I like to call them, the "time capsules of narratives." These cultural centers have preserved historical artifacts, stories, and heritage that could easily have been lost in the dusty pages of inattention.

Walk into any of these museums, and you will be greeted by stories etched in clay, woven in fabric, and carved in wood. You will encounter tales of courage in shackles, resilience in oppression, fierce love in the face of injustice, and a deep-seated sense of identity that refuses to be erased. If we were to air these chronicles on prime time, Netflix might have some serious competition.

But it's not all art, carvings, and museums. One cannot ignore the strides Black women have made in advocating for cultural education and celebration. They have championed the cause of ingraining cultural heritage deeper into our societal fabric. Imagine the education system as an intricate mosaic, and Black women have woven rich threads of cultural heritage into its design, making it colorful and meaningful.

Through these tireless endeavors, multicultural festivities now include soulful African beats that set our feet tapping and exquisite ethnic fashion that has fashion moguls scrambling for their sketchpads. There's a piece of cultural heritage in every classroom and every festival, all courtesy of these unofficial ambassadors of African heritage.

That being said, Black women haven't just stopped at preserving their cultural heritage; they have also been the driving force behind shaping their communities' outlook towards acknowledging, cherishing, and learning from a culture that was once relegated to the fringes. Their endeavors almost remind me of the age-old alchemy of turning a lump of rock into shiny gold, albeit with nuance, charisma, and a glorious head of curls.

Just imagine if Black women got involved in selling real estate. Every apparent 'flaw' of an old house would suddenly be the 'character,' every creaky stair would be wrapped in a tale from the yonder, and every potential buyer would be swayed not by the price tag but by the heartfelt homage to cultural preservation behind the aging facade. Imagine being sold not just walls and a roof but a slice of heritage!

So, it seems like our movie plot has vibrant characters, suspense, drama, emotions, and, most importantly, a beautifully scripted dedication to cultural preservation. Ah! Wait! Did we forget? We are not in a movie plot. This is a reality. It is a glorious reality that has been written and directed by Black women: leaders, fighters, protectors, educators, and most notably, the undying guardians of tradition and identities.

So, while you marvel at Black women's incredible journey in

guarding traditions and identity, remember, they are not done yet. They are still writing, directing, and starring in the real-life blockbuster saga. Only difference? Here, there's no "The End." Here's to learning from and celebrating the beautiful cultural mosaic that Black women weave.

The essence of Black women being guardians of traditions and identities is as eternal as the North Star. And if you are waiting for it to disappear, you might want to invest in a really comfortable chair because it will be a long, long wait.

Remember how your grandma always told you that Black women have been the keepers of stories, the spinners of traditions, and the reservoir of resistance? Well, you better believe her, because these women are not just anyone. They are the generations of powerhouses who took the pain and made it into a mosaic of cultural heritage that rocks the world. Now tell me, isn't that like a Beyoncé concert, where the energy just keeps surging, and the crowd goes wild, except that with our fabulous ladies, it keeps going for centuries?

Just like how you can't appreciate Mona Lisa with just an Instagram filter, you can't genuinely appreciate these women if you're merely tagging along for the ride. Dive in and immerse yourself in their rhythm, vibrant visual arts, mesmerizing dance forms, and wise literature. And when you envelop yourself in these lush layers, you'll see the zeitgeist these women have fought to preserve.

I know it sounds heavy, right? But just like when your mamma told you to eat vegetables because they're good for you, like those greens, acknowledging the rich cultural heritage preserved by Black women and fostering appreciation is good for our society. It's not just about preserving culture; it is also about celebration. It's about hosting the grandest, wildest party for our diverse heritage and making sure it never ends.

But before you dash off and start planning that giant heritage hoedown, stop and think about this: every song, every folk dance, every traditional dish, and yes, even every weave of hair carries within it a story of struggle, resilience, and triumph. So, let's not just be bystanders. Let's be the guardians of these stories; let's make sure they are handed down to the next generation and the next. Let's make sure the world keeps spinning with the sound of their rhythm.

So, are you ready to accept this baton? Remember, the strength of these incredible, indomitable Black women is coursing through our veins. And the world of cultural heritage is ours to protect, preserve, and pass on. So, step up, join the chorus, and add your voice to the symphony. Because, after all, you must admit that life is pretty boring without a little drama, dance, and dynamism.

CONCLUSION

It's wonderful to express gratitude and appreciation. Black women have made immense contributions to various fields, including but not limited to politics, science, literature, the arts, and social justice. Their resilience, strength, and creativity have shaped history and continue to inspire many. Through a comprehensive exploration of their roles as advocates, leaders, caregivers, and cultural influencers, we have witnessed Black women's profound impact on shaping societies and challenging systemic injustices.

From civil rights leaders like Rosa Parks and Fannie Lou Hamer to groundbreaking artists like Maya Angelou and Nina Simone, Black women have played pivotal roles in challenging societal norms and promoting positive change. In contemporary times, figures like Michelle Obama, Kamala Harris, and Ava DuVernay continue to break barriers and serve as role models for future generations.

Beyond the spotlight, countless Black women contribute daily to their communities, families, and workplaces, significantly impacting the world. It's crucial to acknowledge and celebrate their achievements while recognizing the challenges they may face.

This tribute serves as a reminder to appreciate Black women's strength, resilience, and contributions throughout history and in the present. Gratitude fosters understanding and unity, contributing to a more inclusive and equitable society.

The tribute expanded to recognize the unsung heroines who toiled in the shadows, significantly contributing to social justice, education, and the arts. The narrative spotlighted the educators, community organizers, and artists who, despite facing numerous obstacles, played instrumental roles in uplifting their communities and fostering change. Their stories served as a poignant reminder that the impact of Black women extends far beyond the visible realms of history.

As the exploration delved into the modern era, the narrative unfolded to highlight the achievements of contemporary Black women who continue to break barriers and redefine societal norms. From trailblazing political figures like Kamala Harris to influential cultural icons like Beyoncé, Black women have become symbols of empowerment and resilience. Their success stories inspire future generations to dream big and pursue their goals despite facing adversity.

The tribute also addressed the challenges facing Black women today, emphasizing the importance of intersectionality in understanding their unique struggles. Systemic issues such as racial and gender-based discrimination, economic disparities, and healthcare disparities were analyzed to underscore the ongoing battle for equality. By shedding light on these challenges, the narrative aimed to foster a deeper understanding of the multifaceted nature of the Black female experience.

The narrative also explored the concept of allyship and emphasized the importance of solidarity in the fight against injustice. Recognizing that the struggles faced by Black women are interconnected with broader issues of social justice, the tribute called for unity among different communities. By amplifying the voices of Black women and standing alongside them in their pursuit of justice, society can work towards dismantling oppressive systems and creating a more equitable future for all.

As the tribute unfolded, it became evident that Black women have been the unsung architects of change, shaping the course of history through their unwavering determination and resilience. The narrative served as a call to action, urging society to acknowledge and appreciate the immense contributions of Black women, not only during designated months or events but as an integral part of the ongoing narrative of human progress.

In thanking Black women for everything, the tribute recognized that gratitude should be accompanied by tangible efforts to dismantle systemic barriers and create a more just and inclusive world. From policy changes to cultural shifts, the conclusion called for active participation in the ongoing struggle for equality. By focusing on the experiences and voices of Black women, society can move towards a future where every individual, regardless of their background, has the opportunity to thrive.

In essence, "The Blackman's Champion" serves as a comprehensive and heartfelt tribute to Black women, weaving together historical narratives, contemporary achievements, and a vision for a more equitable future. By acknowledging the struggles, celebrating the triumphs, and calling for collective action, the tribute aims to inspire reflection, conversation, and, most importantly, meaningful change. Black women have been and continue to be champions in every sense of the word, and it is incumbent upon us all to ensure that their contributions are not only recognized but actively supported and uplifted for generations to come.

Recognizing the multifaceted roles played by Black women contributes to creating a more inclusive and equitable society where diversity is acknowledged and celebrated. In this spirit of appreciation, we forge a path toward a future where every individual's talent and contribution are recognized, valued, and woven into the fabric of our shared human experience.

REFERENCES

https://zora.medium.com/this-is-how-you-thank-Black-women-e9be2b30e360
https://tvone.tv/videos/mens-tribute-to-women-thank-you-Black-women/
chrome-extension://efaidnbmnnnibpcajpcglclefindmkaj/https://digitalcommons.georgiasouthern.edu/cgi/viewcontent.cgi?article=1552&context=etd
https://www.changegrowlive.org/news/saluting-our-sisters-Black-history-month-our-staff-told-us-about-Black-women-who-have-inspired
chrome-extension://efaidnbmnnnibpcajpcglclefindmkaj/https://web.archive.org/web/20200507034049id_/https://uknowledge.uky.edu/cgi/viewcontent.cgi?article=1006&context=upk_african_american_studies
https://www.linkedin.com/pulse/unveiling-challenges-professional-Black-women-face-derby-davis/
https://www.tandfonline.com/doi/full/10.1080/00131911.2023.2217358
chrome-extension://efaidnbmnnnibpcajpcglclefindmkaj/https://www.apa.org/pubs/journals/releases/tps-tps0000256.pdf
https://www.ncbi.nlm.nih.gov/pmc/articles/PMC10159179/
chrome-extension://efaidnbmnnnibpcajpcglclefindmkaj/https://scholarlycommons.pacific.edu/cgi/viewcontent.cgi?article=5000&context=uop_etds
https://www.proquest.com/openview/0265e52b8b0effa2ca5265d062c491a3/1?pq-origsite=gscholar&cbl=18750
chrome-extension://efaidnbmnnnibpcajpcglclefindmkaj/https://academicworks.cuny.edu/cgi/viewcontent.cgi?article=5185&context=gc_etds
chrome-extension://efaidnbmnnnibpcajpcglclefindmkaj/https://ir.library.illinoisstate.edu/cgi/viewcontent.cgi?article=2252&context=etd

https://www.academia.edu/en/72793059/Resilience_rooted_in_the_earth_stories_of_Black_women_s_survival
https://www.youtube.com/watch?v=BPQBFetX-BA
chrome-extension://efaidnbmnnnibpcajpcglclefindmkaj/https://library.oapen.org/bitstream/handle/20.500.12657/64188/9781628951691.pdf?sequence=1
https://www.ncbi.nlm.nih.gov/pmc/articles/PMC9698362/
chrome-extension://efaidnbmnnnibpcajpcglclefindmkaj/https://fisherpub.sjf.edu/cgi/viewcontent.cgi?article=1380&context=education_etd
https://www.ncbi.nlm.nih.gov/pmc/articles/PMC3072704/
chrome-extension://efaidnbmnnnibpcajpcglclefindmkaj/https://scholarsrepository.llu.edu/cgi/viewcontent.cgi?article=3588&context=etd
chrome-extension://efaidnbmnnnibpcajpcglclefindmkaj/https://scholarworks.waldenu.edu/cgi/viewcontent.cgi?article=13458&context=dissertations
https://www.ncbi.nlm.nih.gov/pmc/articles/PMC6510490/
chrome-extension://efaidnbmnnnibpcajpcglclefindmkaj/https://deepblue.lib.umich.edu/bitstream/handle/2027.42/162987/cspr_1.pdf?sequence=4
https://oxfordre.com/education/display/10.1093/acrefore/9780190264093.001.0001/acrefore-9780190264093-e-1345;jsessionid=31825FD5ABA2F75113C03258340D59F9?rskey=zMj6td&result=9
https://www.sciencedirect.com/science/article/abs/pii/S000187911830109X
https://www.frontiersin.org/articles/10.3389/fmars.2023.1295931/full
chrome-extension://efaidnbmnnnibpcajpcglclefindmkaj/https://thekeep.eiu.edu/cgi/viewcontent.cgi?article=5998&context=theses

https://www.linkedin.com/pulse/harnessing-ai-amplifying-voices-impact-african-women-ngonzi-cfre/
chrome-extension://efaidnbmnnnibpcajpcglclefindmkaj/https://www.unwomen.org/sites/default/files/2023-02/230213%20BLS22613%20UNW%20CSW67.v04%20%282%29.pdf
https://www.linkedin.com/pulse/remarks-minister-higher-education-science/
https://2012-2017.usaid.gov/what-we-do/gender-equality-and-womens-empowerment/addressing-gender-programming/harnessing
https://www.brookings.edu/articles/african-women-and-girls-leading-a-continent/
chrome-extension://efaidnbmnnnibpcajpcglclefindmkaj/https://www.oecd.org/education/ceri/GEIS2016-Background-document.pdf
chrome-extension://efaidnbmnnnibpcajpcglclefindmkaj/https://www.eolss.net/sample-chapters/c03/E1-14-04-04.pdf
https://www.ncbi.nlm.nih.gov/pmc/articles/PMC3222512/
https://www.americanprogress.org/article/top-10-ways-to-improve-health-and-health-equity/
https://studenthealth.uconn.edu/equity/
chrome-extension://efaidnbmnnnibpcajpcglclefindmkaj/https://efina.org.ng/wp-content/uploads/2022/07/Womens-Economic-Empowerment-in-Nigeria-A-critical-look-at-Access.pdf
chrome-extension://efaidnbmnnnibpcajpcglclefindmkaj/https://www.oecd.org/dac/gender-development/47561694.pdf
chrome-extension://efaidnbmnnnibpcajpcglclefindmkaj/https://www.demographic-research.org/volumes/vol47/15/47-15.pdf
chrome-extension://efaidnbmnnnibpcajpcglclefindmkaj/https://docs.gatesfoundation.org/Documents/WomensDigitalFinancialInclusioninAfrica_English.pdf
https://www.today.com/popculture/celebrate-Black-history-4/Black-women-in-history-rcna12963

https://our-ancestories.com/blogs/news/5-Black-women-who-deserve-more-recognition-a-Black-history-month-tribute
https://www.linkedin.com/pulse/honoring-Black-women-history-contributions-robert-f-smith/
https://www.brighton-hove.gov.uk/news/2023/Black-history-month-celebrating-extraordinary-achievements-Black-women
https://www.Blackhistorymonth.org.uk/article/section/african-history/heroines-of-the-horizon-celebrating-the-unveiled-power-of-african-women-in-the-journey-towards-independence/
https://www.ncbi.nlm.nih.gov/pmc/articles/PMC10217808/
chrome-extension://efaidnbmnnnibpcajpcglclefindmkaj/https://scholarsrepository.llu.edu/cgi/viewcontent.cgi?article=3588&context=etd
https://pubmed.ncbi.nlm.nih.gov/7755001/
https://psycnet.apa.org/record/2019-25326-004
https://journals.sagepub.com/doi/full/10.1177/0095798414543014
chrome-extension://efaidnbmnnnibpcajpcglclefindmkaj/https://ir.stthomas.edu/cgi/viewcontent.cgi?article=1100&context=ssw_docdiss
https://medium.com/@ashish006734/the-beauty-of-diversity-redefining-standards-in-the-fashion-and-beauty-industry-5ec690c69214
https://fastercapital.com/content/Redefining-Beauty-Standards--Embracing-Diversity-with-Coveronabounce.html
https://academic.oup.com/kentucky-scholarship-online/book/29233/chapter-abstract/243016836?redirectedFrom=fulltext
chrome-extension://efaidnbmnnnibpcajpcglclefindmkaj/https://cornerstone.lib.mnsu.edu/cgi/viewcontent.cgi?article=1749&context=etds
chrome-extension://efaidnbmnnnibpcajpcglclefindmkaj/https://getd.libs.uga.edu/pdfs/reed_jaleesa_201508_ms.pdf
http://sheisafrica.eu/2018/07/23/10-trail-blazing-african-women-in-sports/
https://www.youthsporttrust.org/news-insight/blogs/shaunagh-brown-Black-history-month
https://www.history.com/topics/Black-history/Black-women-in-sports

https://www.bet.com/article/y9v0fv/trailblazing-Black-women-making-history
https://www.theimpactmagazine.com/lifestyle/bwv/

https://ghana.un.org/en/241006-amplifying-voices-women-and-children-climate-action-maiden-edition-afriwocc-calls-change-and
chrome-extension://efaidnbmnnnibpcajpcglclefindmkaj/https://www.worldbank.org/content/dam/Worldbank/document/Gender/Voice_and_agency_LOWRES.pdf
https://mastercardfdn.org/amplifying-the-voices-of-young-women-for-an-equal-future/
https://docs.lib.purdue.edu/wcj/vol39/iss1/5/
https://nap.nationalacademies.org/read/26834/chapter/7
https://www.epi.org/publication/Black-workers-covid/
https://www.urban.org/urban-wire/you-cant-improve-Black-womens-economic-well-being-without-addressing-both-wealth-and
https://journals.openedition.org/lisa/806
https://www.degruyter.com/document/doi/10.1515/culture-2018-0027/html?lang=en
https://www.scielo.org.za/scielo.php?script=sci_arttext&pid=S1727-37812012000100001
chrome-extension://efaidnbmnnnibpcajpcglclefindmkaj/https://www.diva-portal.org/smash/get/diva2:1224014/FULLTEXT01.pdf

Made in the USA
Columbia, SC
25 April 2024